Attila's Wars, AD 440–53

Hunnic Warrior
VERSUS
Late Roman Cavalryman

COMBAT

Murray Dahm

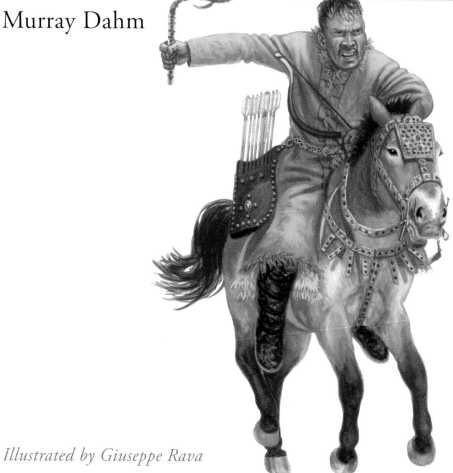

Illustrated by Giuseppe Rava

OSPREY PUBLISHING
Bloomsbury Publishing Plc
Kemp House, Chawley Park, Cumnor Hill, Oxford OX2 9PH, UK
29 Earlsfort Terrace, Dublin 2, Ireland
1385 Broadway, 5th Floor, New York, NY 10018, USA
E-mail: info@ospreypublishing.com
www.ospreypublishing.com

OSPREY is a trademark of Osprey Publishing Ltd

First published in Great Britain in 2022

A catalogue record for this book is available from the British Library.

ISBN: PB 9781472852083; eBook 9781472852038;
ePDF 9781472852021; XML 9781472852045

22 23 24 25 26   10 9 8 7 6 5 4 3 2 1

Maps by www.bounford.com
Index by Rob Munro
Typeset by PDQ Digital Media Solutions, Bungay, UK
Printed and bound in India by Replika Press Private Ltd.

Osprey Publishing supports the Woodland Trust, the UK's leading
woodland conservation charity.

To find out more about our authors and books visit
www.ospreypublishing.com. Here you will find extracts, author
interviews, details of forthcoming events and the option to sign up for
our newsletter.

Author's note

In many works the name of the battle of 451 is given as Catalaunian
Plains, but the battle has many other names: Catalaunian Fields,
Campus Mauriacus, *locus* Mauriacus (*locus* meaning, rather unhelpfully,
'location'), Maurica, Châlons, Troyes. As will become clear, I follow
Jordanes and consider the ridge of the battlefield to be the most
important aspect of the battle, therefore any name that calls the battle
a 'plain' or 'field' or 'campus' seems inappropriate. As such I have taken
Maurica as the name most closely associated with Les Maures Ridge,
identified as modern-day Montgueux by Hughes (2012 and 2019).
Nevertheless, referring to the battle as the Catalaunian Plains (as the
most commonly used name in recent scholarship) is still necessary.
Works on the Huns (and Goths) use some terms interchangeably. For
ease of understanding the smallest grouping of the Huns might be
considered a clan, next a tribe (probably commanded by a leader – a
phylarchos (literally a leader of a tribe; from *phyle,* the Greek for 'tribe').
A combination of tribes (whether a political or military alliance or
other affiliation) shall be considered a nation or a people. In most cases,
however, our sources just make reference to 'Huns' and we are left to
work out how many this means in such cases.

Artist's note

Readers may care to note that the original paintings from which the
colour plates in this book were prepared are available for private sale.
All reproduction copyright whatsoever is retained by the publishers. All
enquiries should be addressed to:

info@g-rava.it

The publishers regret that they can enter into no correspondence upon
this matter.

CONTENTS

Introduction

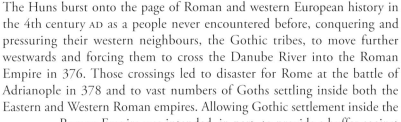

The Huns burst onto the page of Roman and western European history in the 4th century AD as a people never encountered before, conquering and pressuring their western neighbours, the Gothic tribes, to move further westwards and forcing them to cross the Danube River into the Roman Empire in 376. Those crossings led to disaster for Rome at the battle of Adrianople in 378 and to vast numbers of Goths settling inside both the Eastern and Western Roman empires. Allowing Gothic settlement inside the Roman Empire was intended, in part, to provide a buffer against the new threat of the Huns and, in the 4th and early 5th centuries, many men of Gothic descent rose to the highest military offices in both the Eastern and Western Roman empires and did indeed have to fight the Huns.

The origins of the Huns were long regarded as clouded in mystery, but recent work has identified them as a pan-Eurasian phenomenon, probably originating among the lands of the 'steppe nomads' (Kim 2016: 2–4), although Kim prefers the term 'pastoralist' to 'nomad'. This area was not just steppe, however, but a variety of terrain types; it encompassed the five present-day Central Asian republics – Kazakhstan, Kyrgyzstan, Tajikistan, Turkmenistan and Uzbekistan – and Afghanistan, but also stretched to southern Russia, Mongolia, and northern and western China. This vast area encompassed many cultures and at least three language groups (Altaic, Indo-European and Yeniseian). The Huns probably originated with the Xiongnu people (from what is now Mongolia), who appear in Chinese Han Dynasty records from the later 3rd century BC to the early 3rd century AD. This identification was first made in the 18th century and Gibbon accepted the origin, but the theory fell out of favour in the 19th century and later scholars such as

The 5th-century mosaics from the Basilica of Santa Maria Maggiore, Rome, show details of armour, weapons, helmets and tunics that are exactly contemporary with the Roman campaigns against Attila. Note the mix of armour types and helmet designs. (DEA/G. NIMATALLAH/Getty Images)

This silver plaque of a yak, dated to the 1st century AD, comes from the Noin-Ula Burial Site in northern Mongolia (now in the Hermitage Museum, St Petersburg, Russia, Inv. 253). The tombs of the area, situated on the Selenga River and of which there are more than 200, were excavated in 1924–25, and were found to contain burials of the aristocracy of the Xiongnu, probable precursors of the Huns. The graves had been desecrated in antiquity so contained no human remains. (CM Dixon/Print Collector/ Getty Images)

Maenchen-Helfen (1973: 367–75) – he names them Hsiung-nu – remained sceptical. More recently, some (e.g. Fields 2006: 12) have been unwilling to commit to the identification. Kim (2016: 6) reaffirms with certainty that the Xiongnu were the Huns based on more recent evidence. Most ancient authorities link the Huns to the Scythians and trace them back to Herodotus (*The Histories* 1.104, 4.20), writing in the 5th century BC. Ptolemy (*Geography* 3.5.10), writing in the 2nd century AD, mentions a tribe called the Khunnoi – a term that has similarities to the term 'Huns' – and some have latched on to this. No other ancient authority did likewise, however, instead deriving the name used for this people from Herodotus.

The Huns were made up of various tribes who organized themselves in loose confederations until Attila brought more Hunnic nations (and others) under his yoke

This Hephthalite or Kidarite bowl, found in Pakistan and now in the British Museum, London, depicts a Hunnic noble hunting. He is possibly an Alchon, White or Kidara Hun; this view shows clearly his recurve bow in action as well as a *spatha* sword on his left hip. The horse trappings and the horse's short mane are clearly depicted. Jerome, writing in 399, describes the Huns 'speeding here and there on their nimble-footed horses, they were filling all the world with panic and bloodshed' (*Letters* 77.8). Jerome goes on to emphasize the panic they caused: 'everywhere their approach was unexpected, they outstripped rumour in speed, and, when they came, they spared neither religion nor rank nor age' (*Letters* 77.8). Fighting with lassos is also attested – Ammianus' 'twisted cords' (*Res gestae* 31.2.9) – although sometimes such passages are tricky, because the Greek for 'with lassos' is *sokkois* but some manuscripts use the term *sakkois* ('with sacks'). *Sokkois* is a much rarer term, but seems to make more sense than fighting with sacks unless capturing and holding hostages for ransom is meant. Elsewhere, lassos (*laquei*) are mentioned by Vegetius (*De Re Militari* 3.23.3 & 4.23.2). (PHGCOM/Wikimedia/CC BY-SA 3.0)

and, according to one source (Prosper, *Epitoma Chronicon* a.434), forced them into war. The Byzantine emperor Maurice (r. 584–602) observed (*Strategikon* 11.2) that the Huns were ruled by fear of their king, not love. One of the earliest indications that the Huns were a loose confederation of different cultures can be seen in the group of Huns who fought independently with the Goths in the late 370s (Ammianus, *Res gestae* 31.8.4). Independent tribes continued thereafter; John of Antioch writes (*Historia chronike* F187) of the Hun *phylarchoi* ('rulers of tribes') in the raids of the 390s, implying multiple tribes.

The period between around 220 (when the Xiongnu disappear from Chinese sources) and their appearance in Roman historiography in the 370s was long considered a dark age for our knowledge of the Huns. Already in the 3rd century AD, however, there is evidence that they were moving westwards due to military conquest. This thrust westwards continued, the Huns coming into contact with the Sogdians and other cultures at the far eastern edges of Roman knowledge. At the same time, other groups of Huns (such as the White Huns) with cultural and political affinities to the Huns who invaded Europe, moved southwards from Inner Asia. The exact relationships between the different types of Huns – Attila's (European) Huns, Alchon Huns, Xionites, Kidara Huns, the Hephthalites (or White Huns), the Nezak Huns, and the Huna – remain hotly debated, however. As they moved, the Huns absorbed and assimilated cultures rather than displaced them, all of which adds to the complexity of the Huns as never having been a single ethnic or language group.

When Attila and his brother Bleda, and then Attila alone after the death of Bleda, invaded the Roman Empire in 441, 443 and 447, they presented both the Eastern and Western Roman empires with another cataclysmic threat. That threat was only partially dealt with at the battle of the Catalaunian Plains in June 451. Attila would return to devastate northern Italy in 452 and only his death in 453 rescued the Roman Empire from further devastation. Directly or indirectly, therefore, the Huns were responsible for the major crises faced by the Roman Empire in the late 4th and 5th centuries. It was their pressure which caused the Gothic tribes to cross the Danube and the Rhine River into the Roman Empire in overwhelming numbers in the later 4th century and they crossed themselves

The funerary stele of the 4th-century Roman cavalryman Lepontius from Argentoratum (modern-day Strasbourg, France) is one of the last relief funerary monuments created; the tradition of such monuments came to an end soon thereafter. His sword, thrusting spear and round shield are prominent, as are his cloak and helmet. He may be wearing lamellar armour or just a tunic. Now in the Archaeological Museum (Musée Archéologique) of Strasbourg, this copy was made before the original was destroyed during the siege of Strasbourg during the Franco-Prussian War (1870–71). (Wolfgang Sauber/ Wikimedia/CC BY-SA 4.0)

in the 5th century. The Western Roman Empire would never recover and would soon collapse; the Eastern Roman Empire survived and experienced a resurgence of authority under the emperor Justinian I (r. 527–65) and his military commander Belisarius in the 6th century.

The invasions of the Roman Empire by the Huns under Attila spanned almost the entire breadth of both East and West, reaching from Constantinople (modern-day Istanbul, Turkey) in the east to Aurelianum (modern-day Orléans, France) in the west. In many cases we are given very little detail – several sources list 'hundreds' of cities taken and others just state provinces plundered. Other cities may have invented (or exaggerated) their contact with Attila.

The invasion of 441 (**1**) probably crossed at Viminacium (near modern-day Kostolac and Požarevac, Serbia) and the city of Singidunum (modern-day Belgrade, Serbia), capital of the province of Moesia Prima, also fell to the Huns.

The invasion of 443 (**2**) was more extensive. Crossing at Ratiaria (modern-day Arcear, Bulgaria) in the province of Dacia Ripensis, the invaders next moved on Naissus (modern-day Niš, Serbia) on the Nišava River in the province of Dacia Mediterranea. Thereafter, they threatened in all directions – roads led from Naissus to (and from) Lissus (modern-day Lezhë, Albania) via Scupi (modern-day Skopje, North Macedonia) to the south-west, Serdica (modern-day Sofia, Bulgaria) to the east along the *via militaris* ('military road'), Singidunum to the north-west, Thessaloniki (modern-day Thessalonica, Greece) to the south, and Ratiaria to the north-east. This invasion reached Constantinople itself and probably involved the cities between Naissus and Constantinople falling to, or being threatened by, the Huns. We are told they took every fort except Adrianople (modern-day Edirne, Turkey) and Heracleia (Perinthus, near modern-day Mamara Ereğlisi, Turkey). We have detail of the fall of Philippopolis (modern-day Plovdiv, Bulgaria), Arcadiaopolis (modern-day Lüleburgaz, Turkey) and Constantia (probably the fortress opposite Margus (modern-day Požarevac, Serbia). The devastation probably also included the destruction of Nicopolis ad Istrum (modern-day Nikyup, Bulgaria), although this may date to 441 – in which case that invasion was much more extensive than argued here. This path of destruction ran west to east, probably along the *via militaris* from Singidunum on the Danube River, down the Morava River to Constantinople. It passed through a series of important fortified cities such as Viminacium, and then, after Naissus, Serdica and Philippopolis, to Adrianople and on to Constantinople. In 443 we also hear of the Huns advancing towards the Black Sea and the Sea of Marmara and ravaging the Gallipoli peninsula, taking Callipolis (modern-day Gelibolu, Turkey) and Sestus (near modern-day Eceabat, Turkey).

The invasion of 447 (**3**) was a still wider incursion. We are told the Huns ravaged all of the dioceses of Illyricum and Thrace, the provinces of Dacia Ripensis, Dacia Mediterranea, Moesia and Scythia and took the cities and forts of the whole of the province of Europa. Attila may have put Constantinople under siege, but did not take the city. He then made his way through the Balkans and Greece, reaching the pass of Thermopylae (in modern-day Greece) where he was turned back. On his return to the Danube, Attila defeated Arnegisclus at the Utus River (now the Vit River in Bulgaria). Arnegisclus had left Marcianopolis (modern-day Devnya, Bulgaria), the capital of Moesia Secunda in the diocese of Thrace and may have used Storgosia (modern-day Pleven, Bulgaria) as a staging post. Attila was probably aiming to cross the Utus north of Storgosia in order to cross back over the Danube – so north of modern-day Pleven up to modern-day Somovit, Bulgaria, where the two rivers join – perhaps intending to cross at modern-day Calinovăţ Island, Romania.

The invasion of the Western Roman Empire in 451 (**4**) involves more doubt. Attila probably crossed the Rhine at the old Roman fort of Castellum apud Confluentes (modern-day Koblenz, Germany), where the Rhine and the Moselle rivers join. Advancing through Pannonia, he took Divodurum Mediomatricorum (modern-day Metz, France) and other cities claimed to be his victims, including Strasbourg in France and Worms, Mainz, Trier and Cologne in Germany. In Belgium he took Tongres and Tournai, and in France he took Rheims, Cambrai, Thérouanne, Arras, Amiens, Beauvais and Paris. The next destination was Aurelianum, where he was confronted by Roman forces travelling from Mediolanum and Roman allies moving from Tolosa. From there Attila retired towards Tricasses (modern-day Troyes, France) on the Seine River. The location of the battlefield of the Catalaunian Plains is much debated – it is located near Metz, on the Mauriac plain, even on the Loire River (or the Danube) or at a location north, east, or west of Troyes. The ancient town of Catalaunum (modern-day Châlons-en-Champagne, France) was on the Marne River (hence the battle of Châlons), but I have accepted Montgueux, 6km west of Troyes and perhaps known as Les Maures Ridge, as the location of the battle.

The invasion of Italy in 452 (**5**) is likewise shrouded in vaguery. Indeed, all of these invasions are not helped by the fact that we have no idea where the Hunnic capital was located – after each invasion, Attila would retire back to the Danube, but we do not know precisely to where. Several sources suggest that Attila retreated from the Catalaunian Plains into Italy and began the devastation immediately. In 452, Attila again invaded via Pannonia and took several cities in northern Italy, principally, Aquileia (near modern-day Trieste, Italy) and Mediolanum (modern-day Milan, Italy). Other cities are named too: Patavium (modern-day Padua, Italy), Vicentia (modern-day Vicenza, Italy), Verona (modern-day Verona, Italy), Brixia (modern-day Brescia, Italy), Bergamum (modern-day Bergamo, Italy) and Ticinum (modern-day Pavia, Italy). The cities that were attacked may also have included Bellunum (modern-day Belluno, Italy), although Travisium (modern-day Treviso, Italy) seems to have been spared. Attila stopped his advance where the Mincius River (now the Mincio River in Italy) flowed into the Padum River (now the Po River in Italy). This will have been near what was (and is) Mantua, past which the Mincius flowed. Nearly all the sources tell us that Attila planned on taking Rome itself, but this seems an unlikely destination. The Western Roman emperor, Valentinian III (r. 425–55), may have evacuated his capital at Ravenna and the Roman army may have been kept at Bononia (modern-day Bologna, Italy) to block a passage through the Apennines towards Rome during the invasion of 452.

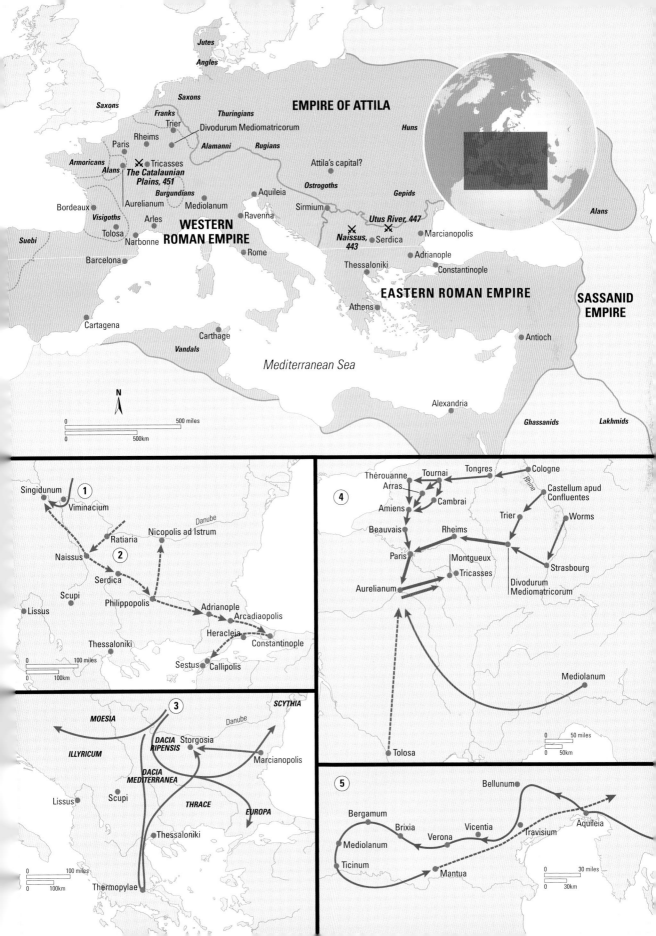

Jutes

Angles

Saxons

Saxons

EMPIRE OF ATTILA

Franks
Trier

Thuringians

Divodurum Mediomatricorum

Rheims

Huns

Paris

Alamanni

Rugians

Attila's capital?

Armoricans

Alans ✕ Tricasses

The Catalaunian Plains, 451

Ostrogoths

Gepids

Alans

Burgundians

Aquileia

Aurelianum

Mediolanum

Sirmium

✕ *Utus River, 447*

Bordeaux

Ravenna

Visigoths

Arles

✕ *Naissus, 443*
Serdica

Marcianopolis

Tolosa

Narbonne

WESTERN ROMAN EMPIRE

Rome

Adrianople

Suebi

Barcelona

Thessaloniki

Constantinople

EASTERN ROMAN EMPIRE

SASSANID EMPIRE

Cartagena

Athens

Carthage

Vandals

Antioch

Mediterranean Sea

N

Alexandria

Ghassanids

Lakhmids

0   500 miles
0   500km

1

Singidunum

Viminacium

Naissus

2

Ratiaria

Danube

Nicopolis ad Istrum

Scupi

Serdica

Lissus

Philippopolis

Adrianople

Arcadiaopolis

Heracleia

Constantinople

Thessaloniki

Sestus
Callipoli

0   100 miles
0   100km

3

SCYTHIA

MOESIA

Danube

DACIA RIPENSIS
Storgosia

ILLYRICUM

DACIA MEDITERRANEA

Marcianopolis

Lissus

Scupi

THRACE

EUROPA

Thessaloniki

Thermopylae

0   100 miles
0   100km

4

Thérouanne
Tournai
Tongres
Cologne

Arras

Castellum apud Confluentes

Amiens

Cambrai

Rhine

Beauvais

Rheims

Trier

Worms

Paris

Montgueux

Tricasses

Aurelianum

Strasbourg

Divodurum Mediomatricorum

Mediolanum

Tolosa

0   50 miles
0   50km

5

Bellunum

Bergamum

Brixia

Vicentia

Aquileia

Verona

Travisium

Mediolanum

Ticinum

Mantua

0   30 miles
0   30km

The Opposing Sides

ARMY COMPOSITION AND SIZE

Hunnic

For many aspects of Hun culture we are hamstrung by our sources which, although plentiful, are often fragmentary and do not provide modern historians with the level of detail we would prefer. Often our sources' information is vague or inaccurate (where we can tell) and, even when a source was in a position to give us precise details – such as Cassiodorus, Olympiodorus or Priscus, who were all sent on embassies to the Huns – they often do not satisfy our modern requirements. They are all we have, however, and although aspects of archaeology continue to add to our knowledge, we must use what we have to our best ability.

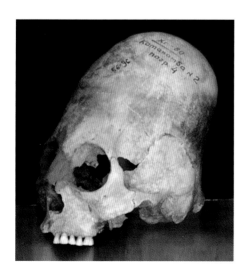

Jordanes tells us (*Getica* 182) that just before the battle of the Catalaunian Plains, Attila's army numbered 500,000 men. No modern authority comes close to believing such a figure (although Syvänne uses it). This massive number is, however, also consistent with the huge losses attributed to the Catalaunian Plains fighting: 165,000 in Jordanes (*Getica* 217), 300,000 in Hydatius (*Chronicle* Olympiad 308/28) and 180,000 in Paul the Deacon (*Historia Romana* 14.6). When the Goths crossed the Danube in 376, we are told by Eunapius (*Historia* F42) that they numbered 200,000 men. John Malalas states (*Chronicle* 358/14.10) that Attila had many tens of thousands of men, so too the *Chronicon Paschale* (Olympiad 307, 450). The purpose of these numbers is to emphasize the overwhelming horde-like nature of these enemies. There are many losses to the

Huns that are only hinted at in the sources, but defeat seems to have been a common feature. Luckily for the Romans, they could always purchase peace with gold – but the price was ever increasing.

We find other observations in the ancient sources that may be useful for estimating the strength of the Huns in general terms. Ammianus describes (*Res gestae* 31.2.21–22) the Halani as being similar to the Huns, growing up in the saddle: all men were warriors and they delighted in danger and war. This picture is confirmed by Sidonius (*Carmina* 2.262–70), although in somewhat poetic terms: he tells us that Hun children were born for battle, and scarcely had they learned to stand,

This portrait of the Alchon Hun king Khingila (r. 440–90), a contemporary of Attila's, on a Hunnic coin clearly shows skull elongation. Ammianus, Jordanes and others also refer to cheek scarring among Hunnic males, but there is no evidence of this in such portraits and other depictions. Jordanes tells us that the Huns possessed the 'cruelty of wild beasts' (*Getica* 128) and cut the cheeks of their males with a sword to inure them to wounds. Ammianus records (*Res gestae* 31.2.2) that at birth the cheeks of the males are marked by an iron. Thus, they did not grow beards and, as Jordanes tells us, 'are short in stature, quick in bodily movement, alert horsemen, broad shouldered, ready in the use of bow and arrow, and have firm-set necks which are ever erect in pride' (*Getica* 128). Others such as Jerome (*Commentary on Isaiah* 7:20–21) fixate on this supposed facial cutting and the inability of the Huns to grow beards. (PHGCOM/Wikimedia/CC BY-SA 3.0)

they were put on the back of a horse. Whatever the numbers of men, women and children involved in Hun migrations, it is probable that male children were inducted into warfare relatively early and probably continued to fight for many years. Skill in archery was clearly taught from a young age and maintained. Although we lack detail about the Huns, earlier cultures enrolled boys young and the ages of military service were often assumed to span the years from 18 to 60, but there are exceptions both younger and older. For some commentators, the number of 200,000 or 500,000 represents the entire people of Huns or Goths and so, in terms of fighting men, the number would be considered slightly below half of that. Even so, those are still massive numbers of men to move, feed and coordinate on a battlefield and other historians bring the estimates of manpower down lower still.

The entries of Prosper in his *Epitoma Chronicon* that mention Attila and the Huns are often brief, although they present fascinating summations of our information. Prosper records (*Epitoma Chronicon* a.451) that, after Attila killed Bleda and forced his brother's people to submit to him, he was thus strengthened by the resources of the deceased Bleda, and Attila forced many thousands of the neighbouring peoples into war. Prosper praises the foresight of the Roman general Aëtius in 451 in gathering a force of allies hurriedly collected from everywhere that matched the numbers of the Huns. This praise implies that indeed, the Huns usually outnumbered any force the Romans could muster against them. Although modern scepticism towards ancient sources is useful, especially with regard to numbers, every source mentions the huge numbers of men at the Catalaunian Plains so, perhaps, we should entertain the possibility that there were indeed huge numbers involved. More than that, if an unprecedented alliance was needed to match the Huns' numbers at the Catalaunian Plains, it is not difficult to imagine that the Huns nearly always outnumbered their Roman opponents in previous battles.

Riding a Takhi horse with its characteristic short mane and tail, a young Hunnic aristocrat cavalryman charges towards the breached walls of Naissus in 443. The Hunnic siege platforms, rams and ladders have done their work and the city lies open. Eager to prove his worth to his fellows, he leads the apparently reckless charge from the front.

Naissus, AD 443

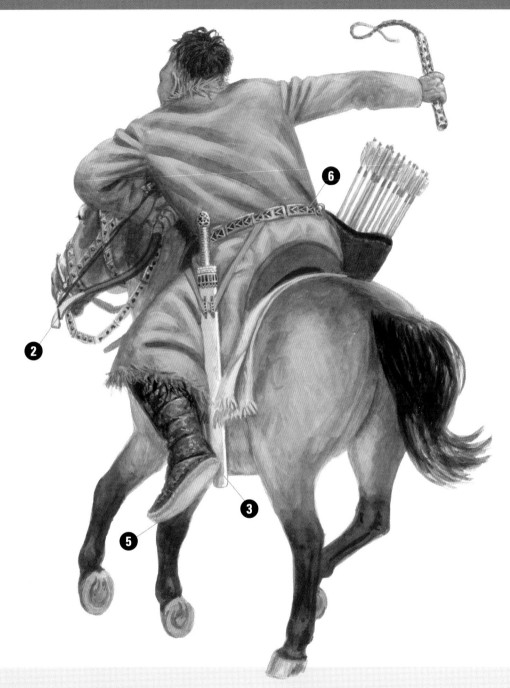

Weapons, dress and equipment

Our cavalryman rides with his bow and reins in his left hand and flourishes his horsewhip (**1**), used to control his horse in the absence of spurs, in his right hand. He is armed with a composite bow (**2**) and a *spatha* (**3**) – taken from a fallen foe – at his left side. He wears a thick tunic (**4**), and typical boots (**5**), and a belt (**6**) made of gold and decorated with garnets. He is equipped with a bowcase quiver (**7**), unusually on his right hip.

His head shows evidence of skull elongation, practised by aristocratic and royal families among the various peoples of the Huns. He also shows the beginnings of a moustache; the inability of the Huns to grow beards was a trait remarked upon in the sources. Our sources record that Hun cavalry charges appeared chaotic (at least to Roman eyes) until the last moment when the disparate groups of cavalry suddenly coordinated to arrive and deliver their charge in unison.

Roman

The Roman Army of the mid-5th century is not described in our sources in the detail we have for earlier centuries. The ancient historians of the Romans' wars against the Huns do not provide us with details of which units were involved in battles. Often we only get the name of the commander, and we must combine our sources to try to understand which command they held; and the descriptions often do not differentiate as to whether an army deployed cavalry, infantry or a mixture of units. The Roman generals Arnegisclus in 447 and Aëtius in 451 are two such cases; the former is called *magister militum* ('master of soldiers'), meaning either he was the *magister utriusque militiae* or *magister militum per Thracias* (the latter probably held a similar supreme command as *comes et magister utriusque militiae* although no source tells us as much). Other commanders are called *dux* or *comes*, which can give us some clues. These titles, used in conjunction with the detail in the *Notitia Dignitatum* (*The List of Offices*), a listing (in two separate halves) of Roman civil and military posts, tell us what position a commander had and therefore suggest what troops he may have had at his immediate disposal.

The armies of the Roman Empire in the 5th century were still divided into armies of *limitanei* (sing. *limitaneus*), troops who manned the borders of the Roman Empire and who were stationed in a particular border province, and more mobile armies called *comitatenses* (sing. *comitatus*), which were based in a particular (usually central) city and able to respond to a particular threat. The men in these armies were resident in particular towns and their positions became hereditary, sons enlisting in the units of their fathers. This division had been introduced in the late 3rd and 4th centuries and was still in place in the 5th century. There had been changes during that timeframe and some units had been moved around the Roman Empire, but we are not sure of the exact permutations of these changes or movements. Both the

Augmented during the reign of the Eastern Roman emperor Theodosius II (r. 408–50), the walls of Constantinople were able to withstand a Hunnic siege, though Callinicus tells us (*Life of Saint Hypatius* 104) that the population of the city fled in fear. As Attila had shown he could take cities, the Romans' fear of Constantinople falling was real indeed. (DEA/G. DAGLI ORTI/Getty Images)

limitanei and *comitatenses* armies included units termed *legiones* (legions), *auxilia* (auxiliary forces) and *vexillationes* (detachments), although they were of different strengths – but these strengths can only be estimates because we are not given unit strengths in our sources. The *vexillationes* were cavalry, although in *limitanei* armies cavalry could also be called *alae* (sing. *ala*, 'wing') or *cunei* (sing. *cuneus*, 'wedge'). The term *cuneus* may be misleading, however, perhaps only meaning an irregular unit of cavalry rather than the description of a tactical formation.

Using the *Notitia Dignitatum* we can estimate which units would have been available for the commanders at Naissus, the Utus and the Catalaunian Plains. This is a less-than-ideal scenario, however. The two halves of the *Notitia Dignitatum* describe the troops available in the two halves of the Roman Empire, but its description and detail are far from complete. The two halves were also written at different times – the description of the Eastern Roman Empire army probably dates from *c*.390 and the Western Roman Empire section probably dates from *c*.425. Some of the information in the *Notitia Dignitatum*, however, stretches back into the 4th century – such as Roman Army units based in Britain, which traditionally was considered to have been abandoned in 410 or 411 (Zosimus, *Nea Historia* 6.10.2). Recent discoveries in Britain, however, have suggested a much longer Roman presence into the 450s. The *Notitia Dignitatum* is therefore a snapshot of a moment (or two moments) in time, not necessarily a document that reveals a precise system in place for a number of decades. Nevertheless, it gives us our best opportunity to estimate the forces available to any commander and those involved in each encounter.

Unit strengths are also difficult to estimate. Usually, legions are estimated at 1,000 men and cavalry units at 500 men (such as the units of the *scholae*). Other commentators have estimated the strength of *limitanei* legions to have been only 500 men and cavalry units to have numbered 300, but some cavalry units had an actual strength of only 80–160 men.

Circitor of the *Equites sagittarii iuniores*

Inside the walls of Naissus a junior officer of horse-archers reacts to the breach in the city's walls. He is from one of the units of *vexillationes comitatenses* commanded by the *magister militum per Thracias*, a member of the *Equites sagittarii iuniores*. Usually tasked with defending the arms factory (*fabrica*) located in the city, he has been given a desperate mission to summon aid to the small garrison of Naissus from Serdica. He is not to know that Serdica is the Huns' next target.

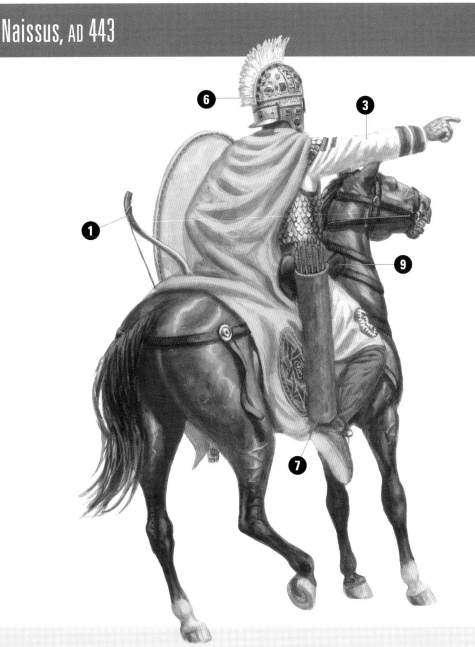

Weapons, dress and equipment

Our cavalryman is armed with a bow (**1**) and also wears a *spatha* at his left hip (**2**). He wears a typical long-sleeved decorated lined tunic (**3**) and a cloak (**4**). He eschews greaves, but wears scale armour (**5**) with a collar and a Berkasovo-type cavalry ridge-helmet (**6**). Despite its outwardly expensive appearance, most of the decorations are glass and the helmet is iron covered in silver-gilt.

He is equipped with a quiver (**7**) and carries his shield (**8**) displaying the blazon of his unit. No shield designs for eastern cavalry units are depicted in the *Notitia Dignitatum*, so this shield design is taken from a (rare) tombstone of a cavalryman from the same unit (*AE* 1976, 00617) found at Tomis (modern-day Constanța, Romania) in 1913. His horse has a four-pommel saddle (**9**) and wears no chamfron to cut down on weight.

Our best evidence of the junior officers in Roman armies of the 4th and 5th centuries comes from a speech of Jerome (*Against John of Jerusalem* 19), which lists the pay grades of various ranks; these pay grades may not be the same as the ranks themselves, however. The list is corroborated by a 5th-century edict issued by the Eastern Roman emperor Justinian I (r. 527–65) in 534 (*Codex Justinianus* I.27.2:19-3). These pay grades, in order, were: *tiro* ('recruit'), *eques* or *pedes* ('cavalryman' or 'infantryman'), *semissalis*, *circitor*, *biarchus*, *centenarius*, *ducenarius*, *senator*, *primicerius* and *tribunus*. The standard pay for a cavalry *semissalis*, *circitor*, *biarchus* or *centenarius* was the same: one *capitus* (the equivalent of 20 *solidi* or one year's horse fodder).

ORGANIZATION AND COMMAND

Hunnic

Attila ruled a vast polyglot tribal empire centred on eastern and central Europe for a relatively short period, from around 434 to his death in 453. He was probably around 50 years of age (perhaps older) when he invaded Roman territory in the 440s although some make him younger, born in about 406; we do not know his age for certain. Until his sole rule (*c*.444/45–53), the Huns were ruled by an unusual dual kingship of brothers, which Attila shared with his elder brother Bleda until 444/45. Bleda and Attila had inherited the Hunnic kingship from their uncles, Octar and Ruga; Octar died in 430 and Ruga in 434. The new kings seem to have made an alliance to stay away from Roman territory as early as 435. Instead, the Huns moved against the Sorgosi, possibly the Sassanid Persian Empire, but they were repulsed. They invaded Roman territory in 441 (when the terms of their previous treaty expired or had not been met), crossing into the Roman provinces of Illyricum and Moesia.

A year of peace followed. In 442 or, more likely, 443 the Huns invaded Roman territory again and successfully took Naissus (modern-day Niš, Serbia) by siege. Later in 443 they invaded again and turned against the Eastern Roman emperor Theodosius II (r. 408–50), in Constantinople. The Huns inflicted a defeat on the Eastern Roman armies and Theodosius II sued for peace, paying a huge indemnity of 6,000lb (2,700kg) of gold as well as agreeing to an additional yearly tribute of 2,100lb for four years. The Huns, satisfied, then withdrew back across the Danube. Bleda died soon after this – Jordanes (*Getica* 181), Prosper and Marcellinus Comes all speculate that he was murdered by his brother – and Attila took control as sole king.

Although the sources emphasize the role and attributes of Attila as king of the Huns, it is clear that many tribal groups made up the Hunnic nation and that these usually fought in tribal groups commanded by the chieftains. In many cases such tribal groups were attractive allies for the Romans and were hired by both the Eastern and Western Roman empires to fight as *foederati* ('allies'; from *foedus*, 'treaty') (Eunapius, *Historia* F60). Although the Huns are very often described as nomads, Priscus refers (*History* F11.2 & F11.3) to Attila's capital – which he visited in *c*.448 – as a 'large village'. The location of this capital has never been established, however, but its very existence shows that the notion of purely nomadic Huns is misplaced. Even Ammianus and others describe the wagon laagers of the Goths and Huns, although the idea that there was a permanent settlement to which the Huns retired after each invasion is suggested rather than explicit. Steppe villages (*pusztas*) did exist, so even the idea of steppe nomads is misplaced and Ammianus' idea that they knew no roof (*Res gestae* 31.2.4) is just wrong.

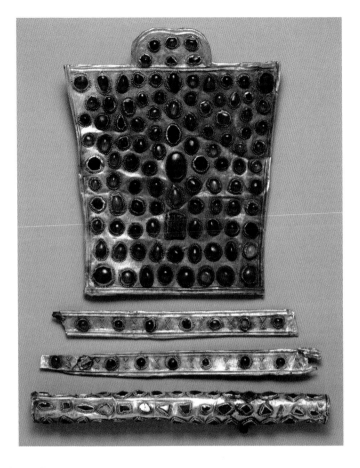

These Hunnic horse trappings, now in the Walters Art Museum, Baltimore, were found in southern Russia. They include a chamfron (the large shape) and bridle mounts; the tube is a horsewhip handle. The style is typically Hunnic, with gold work decorated with beaded stones. (Walters Art Museum/ Wikimedia/Public Domain)

Olympiodorus of Thebes includes information on Hun organization, probably witnessed at first hand in 412 when he went on an embassy to the Hun king Donatus – a king only he mentions. He does, however, distinguish (*Gle Syggrathes* F18) between the singular leader of a confederacy of tribes (*phylarchos* – 'the chief' or 'commander') and the leader of an individual tribe (*rex*). It was noted above that John of Antioch writes (*Historia chronike* F187) of the Hun *phylarchoi* ('rulers of tribes') in the raids of the 390s, implying the existence of multiple tribes. Marcellinus Comes also mentions (*Chronicle* 441) Bleda and Attila as being kings (*reges*). Ammianus tells us (*Res gestae* 31.2.7) that each group was led by a 'first' or 'leading man' (*primates*). Olympiodorus also writes of Hunnic retainers (*oikeioi*) and captains (*lochagoi*); the use of these standard Greek terms perhaps gives us some sense of how Hunnic command structures worked. In the same fragment, Olympiodorus also writes (*Gle Syggrathes* F19) of kings whose archery skills he admired; and of the one 'first king' (*regon protos*). Attila, therefore, was probably both the *regon protos* and the *phylarchos*. Priscus uses more vague terminology (he is inaccurate on Roman and Greek titles too) and his use of the terms 'Scythian' and 'Royal Scythians' (*basileon Skytheon* – *History* F9.4) to describe the royal families of the Huns has introduced much confusion into the matter of Hunnic origins. The term was used by Herodotus (*The Histories* 4.20), whom Priscus may have copied, and then shows up in Zosimus (*Nea Historia* 4.20.3) and elsewhere. Priscus (*History* F11.1) calls Edeco one of Attila's most trusted

This fibula of a cicada, now in the Hungarian National Museum (Magyar Nemzeti Muzeum) in Budapest shows typical features of Hunnic art using gold and garnets. Other examples can be found in silver and only gold. The pin and spring to attach the cloak are underneath the design. The repetition of cicada motifs suggests, perhaps, that a cicada was a mark of rank or had other important symbolism in Hunnic society. Similar designs were taken up by the Franks and Merovingians. (CM Dixon/ Print Collector/Getty Images)

men and an intimate; in F11.2 he is called one of the leading warriors. Later, in the same fragment, Priscus notes that Edeco, Orestes and Scottas and others of the 'picked men' (*logades*) came to the Roman ambassadors. The term *logades* was usually used when referring to elite units and might suggest the same in a Hunnic context, perhaps denoting Attila's guards or an elite warrior unit. Given that these men went on embassies and met another embassy, however, it may indicate that they were picked and trusted leaders, especially given the description of Edeco as a leading warrior. It is not much to go on, but it is possible. In all, five *logades* are named by Priscus; in addition to Edeco, Orestes and Scottas we have Onegesius and Berichus. Elsewhere we find the five men mentioned as a group, which might imply that they were a unit or that we can consider them as a group of officers.

Vegetius (*De Re Militari* 1.20) tells us that the Romans had learned much from the Huns and Alans regarding horsemanship. Vegetius also recognized that the archery of the Goths, Halani and Huns had taught the Romans a thing or two. There must have been unit organizations, perhaps even with specific battlefield roles, but we do not have details of them.

Although we remain ignorant of Hunnic units and exact command structures other than (on occasion) the names of the commanders of groups of warriors, the troops themselves seem to have fought to impress their leaders and to gain renown and reward from their commanders. This is an ascribed motivation for tribal warfare that goes back to Tacitus in the 1st century AD describing the Germanic tribes (*Germania* 14), but we do find the Huns and their allies behaving in the same way.

Roman

The army of the Roman Empire in the 440s and 450s was, in many ways, the same as the army of the late 4th century. Indeed, some of our evidence (such as the *Notitia Dignitatum* and Vegetius) comes (or may come) from the 5th century and so could be a better representation of that century than the earlier one, although it must be used as evidence for the 4th century too. What is more, institutional change was relatively slow and so it should be no surprise if the Roman Army was similar.

In 447, Arnegisclus is called *magister militum* or *magister utriusque militiae*; as such he would have had several cavalry units at his command. Seven units are listed in the *Notitia Dignitatum* for the *magister militum per Thracias*: the *Comites Arcadiaci*, the *Comites Honoriaci*, the *Equites Theodosiaci iuniores*, the *Equites catafractarii Albigenses*, the *Equites sagittarii seniores*, the *Equites sagittarii iuniores* and the *Equites primi Theodosiani*. These unit names suggest that Arnegisclus had all manner of cavalry types at his command, from horse-archers (*sagittarii*) to heavily armed (*catafractarii*); most, however,

were cavalry units without designation of a type, so we can assume these were 'medium' cavalry armed with thrusting spears and shields and capable of mêlée combat. The proportion of troops represented in armies by these types of Roman cavalry varied; heavily armoured cavalry (*cataphractii* and *clibanarii*) accounted for 15 per cent, horse-archers and missile cavalry 25 per cent and medium cavalry 60 per cent.

It is possible that other units from the *magister militum Praesentalis* I and II (the 'master of soldiers in the imperial presence') were also called in by Arnegisclus; each army had a further 12 cavalry units although, as these were armies for fighting in the emperor's presence, it is uncertain if they would have been seconded to a *magister militum*. We do, however, have evidence of *vexillationes* of *palatini* (palace troops) units in *comitatus* armies, such as the three *palatini vexillationes* in the *comitatus* of the *magister militum per Thracias*. So, it is entirely possible Aëtius later had some such units with him from imperial armies – and the proportion of cavalry units in those armies was higher and therefore could provide Aëtius with the mobile troops he doubtless needed.

Estimates of the size of the Late Roman Army are usually divided into 'large' and 'small' camps. Writing in the 6th century, Agathias estimates (*Histories* 5.13.7–8) that the Roman Army in the 'old days' – probably the reign of the emperor Constantine I (r. 306–37) – numbered 645,000 men. Zosimus (*Nea Historia* 2.15.1–2 & 2.22.1–2) recorded that the Roman Army numbered 581,000 men in total during the first quarter of the 4th century. Although some modern-day commentators argue that Roman Army numbers remained consistently high, other scholars posit that the troop levels cited by the ancient authors are theoretical numbers that do not reflect the realities of units in the field; accordingly, such commentators revise the number of men down to a total of 400,000 or thereabouts. In the battles examined in this study, I have argued for higher estimates of troops involved on both sides, especially for the Catalaunian Plains where it is clear that a large Roman alliance was brought to bear against an equally large alliance of Huns and others. The sheer scale of that battle and the vast number of casualties on both sides are emphasized by all of the surviving sources.

ABOVE LEFT
A panel from the so-called Stilicho sarcophagus. Situated in the Basilica of Sant'Ambrogio, Milan, it offers remarkable details of dress and manners. Here we can see bearded soldiers at left and clean-shaven men wearing Phrygian caps to the right of a statue on a column. Note the tunics, cloaks, leggings and variety of hairstyles. (Sailko/Wikimedia/CC BY 3.0)

ABOVE RIGHT
Another panel from the Stilicho sarcophagus. Note the Chi-Ro symbol, so similar to many of the shield designs depicted in the *Notitia Dignitatum*, and the Alpha and Omega flanking the symbol. Note also the clearly crenelated battlements behind the standing figures – these are the kinds of walls Attila breached in the sieges of Naissus, Aquileia and other cities although the larger walls of Constantinople kept him out. (Sailko/Wikimedia/CC BY 3.0)

By the time of the *Notitia Dignitatum*, the Eastern Roman Empire's armies consisted of approximately 104,000 men in the *comitatenses* and *palatini* units, 3,500 in the *scholae* (elite guards) units and 195,000 troops in the *limitanei*. In the Western Roman Empire's armies, the *comitatenses* and *palatini* units could field approximately 98,000 men, the *scholae* consisted of 2,500 men and the *limitanei* could contribute a further 54,000 men. About one-third of the units listed in the *Notitia Dignitatum* are cavalry units; they probably contained fewer men than infantry units, however, and cavalry probably made up only around 20 per cent of *comitatus* armies. Using these numbers, the total number of cavalry was relatively small – 20,000 in the *comitatenses* and *palatini* units of the Eastern Roman Empire's armies, slightly fewer in those of the Western Roman Empire.

Using the overall breakdown of percentages of units that appear to be heavy cavalry, horse-archers or medium cavalry, we can reconstruct these cavalry compositions in more detail. Therefore, of Arnegisclus' force of 8,000 cavalry, 1,200 may have been heavy cavalry, 2,000 horse-archers and missile cavalry and the remaining 4,800, medium cavalry. At the Catalaunian Plains, Aëtius' approximately 10,000 Roman cavalry may have comprised 1,500 heavy cavalry, 2,500 horse-archers and missile cavalry and 6,000 medium cavalry. If the Visigoths under Thorismund (Jordanes calls him 'Thorismud'), son of Theodoric I, matched this number and these proportions, 20,000 cavalry opposed the charge of the Huns. When Theodoric I, king of the Visigoths (r. 418–51), rode to support those Visigoths already engaged, he will have joined with the remaining Visigothic cavalry, the organization of these troops perhaps conforming to the *scholae* model employed by the Romans.

These numbers must remain estimates, however; Syvänne (2020: 100–01), using Paul the Deacon (*Historia Romana* 13.4), Jordanes and Sidonius, calculates 'conservative' estimates of the forces much higher than these numbers. He estimates a Hunnic army of Huns and allies of 410,000 men, with 265,000 cavalry and 145,000 infantry; and for the Romans, 36,500 cavalry and 100,000 infantry. Syvänne adds the army of Illyricum – some 43,000 men – to Aëtius' forces: 12,500 from the *comitatus* and 30,500 from the *limitanei*. He has Aëtius bring 15,000 *bucellarii* (private heavy escort cavalry paid for by the commander himself) from Italy. For Syvänne, the allied force consists of massive numbers: 60,000 Visigothic cavalry, 60,000 Alan cavalry and other allies to make up the total of 500,000. The precision he assumes from the evidence available is highly doubtful, however, but he comes close to the number of 500,000 men for the Huns related by Jordanes, and his guesses for the *foederati* come to a similar figure for the Romans and their allies. Although unattested in the sources, Aëtius may indeed have also had a unit of *bucellarii*. Such units became much more common in the 6th century as private cavalry forces used by commanders, but the term was used with regularity from the reign of the emperor Honorius (r. 393–423) (Olympiodorus, *Gle Syggrathes* F74). A single unit of *bucellarii* is listed in the *Notitia Dignitatum*, the *Bucellarii iuniores* (their exact title is not entirely clear), a *comitatenses* vexillation under the *Magister Militum per Orientem*. This unit was not an outfit that had been privately raised and paid for as they would become, however,

but was listed in the regular army. Syvänne having Aëtius bring 15,000 *bucellarii* from Italy (2020: 100–01) does not correspond with Sidonius (*Carmina* 7.329–35), who states that Aëtius left Italy with no legionaries, and only a few meagre *auxilia* – no mention of *bucellarii* and certainly not a massive force of 15,000.

Jordanes tells us that the foresight of Aëtius meant that he had gathered a mass of men to meet the Huns on 'equal terms' (*Getica* 191). This implies the presence of a large number of cavalry on the Roman/allied side, or that – if we take these low numbers combined – we arrive at a lower estimate of the Huns' capability as well. If Aëtius had 10,000 cavalry and his allies brought similar numbers, maybe up to a total of 50,000 Roman/allied cavalry, it might imply that the Hun strength was similar to that number. It is not the 500,000 men of Jordanes, but a cavalry battle involving 100,000 horsemen is still unbelievably massive (but in keeping, perhaps, with the hyperbole).

These horses and riders from the Great Hunt Mosaic, Villa Romana del Casale, Piazza Armerina, Sicily, show Roman horse trappings and details of dress including tunics, leggings, shoes and cloaks. The shields seem to be of the same design as military ones, although these designs do not exactly match any of those depicted in the *Notitia Dignitatum*. (DEA/ARCHIVIO J. LANGE/Getty Images)

EQUIPMENT AND TACTICS

Hunnic

We must rely on the historians of the 4th century, and the earliest western observers of the Huns, for several observations on their tactics. In some cases, these observations accord with later accounts although in others they are unique.

Ammianus introduces the Huns early in book 31 of his histories as almost inseparable from their horses, living on them night and day, and were not suited to battle on foot, instead fighting exclusively as cavalry (*Res gestae* 31.2.6). This last point is misinformed, although the Romans of the late 4th century encountered Huns exclusively as cavalry. Zosimus also tells us (*Nea Historia* 4.20.4) that the Huns were ignorant and incapable of fighting on foot, but employed methods such as wheeling, charging, retreating and shooting from their horses, thereby wreaking immense slaughter. Maurice states (*Strategikon* 11.2) that the Hunnish peoples begin to form their battle line during the night so that it is ready in the morning, forming a line of irregular units which has the appearance of a single battle line (unlike the three he recommends for Roman armies). Ammianus informs us (*Res gestae* 31.2.8) that the Huns formed *cuneatim* ('wedge-shaped') masses with their cavalry, lightly armed for quick action, and that they could divide with unexpected rapidity while in action and then attacked rapidly in bands deploying missiles (arrows and javelins) as well as using cloth plaited into nooses. Olympiodorus records (*Gle Syggrathes* F19) that the Hunnic kings had a natural talent for archery. Ammianus describes the apparent disorder of the Hun cavalry charges (actually evidence of their exquisite horsemanship); the Huns could deal great slaughter using such tactics, which the Romans were unable to counter effectively. Ammianus does not hesitate to call them 'the most terrible of all warriors' (*Res gestae* 31.2.9), fighting from a distance with missiles with bone points. Jordanes calls the Huns 'fiercer than ferocity itself' (*Getica* 121). Their hand-to-hand fighting was waged without a care for their own safety and, in addition to swords, they also used plaited ropes tied into nooses to entangle their enemies.

Ammianus describes (*Res gestae* 31.2.5) Hun clothing as made of linen or of the skins of field mice; a tunic, once put around their neck is never taken off until it disintegrates. On their heads are round caps and on their 'shaggy' legs are the skins of kid-goats. According to Ammianus (*Res gestae* 31.2.6), Hun shoes were not made with lasts and so were shapeless, and this was the reason Huns were not well suited to infantry battles. Huns were therefore 'nearly always on horseback, their horses being ill-shaped, but hardy' and they could sit side-saddle if required: 'There is not a person in the whole nation who cannot remain on his horse day and night' (*Res gestae* 31.2.6). Everything took place on horseback; buying and selling, sleeping, councils. Ammianus goes on to tell us that, when Huns go into battle,

> ... they form in a solid body, and utter all kinds of terrific yells. They are very quick in their operations, of exceeding speed, and fond of surprising their enemies. With a view to this, they suddenly disperse, then reunite, and again,

after having inflicted vast loss upon the enemy, scatter themselves over the whole plain in irregular formations: always avoiding a fort or entrenchment. (*Res gestae* 31.2.8)

This is perhaps one of the most useful descriptions we have of Hun tactics, which comes in an ethnographical digression on the Huns in the context of their contact with the Goths in 375. What is more, the term Ammianus uses for 'solid body' is *cuneus*, meaning a wedge. Such formations had been employed by Roman armies since the 1st century AD and Ammianus mentions their use (*Res gestae* 31.9.3) in the later 370s. Wedge formations were used in infantry tactics too (Ammianus *Res gestae* 17.13.9; Vegetius, *De Re Militari* 3.19). In this case, however, *cuneus* may not mean wedge at all but instead be a description of a group (hence 'solid body' as the translation). In the *Notitia Dignitatum* (Orientis 39.1–9) we find *cunei* used as a description of some irregular auxiliary cavalry units – 49 such units are mentioned and 48 of them are cavalry units. The term may have been a looser term than *ala* ('wing'; pl. *alae*) or *turma* ('squadron'; pl. *turmae*), and therefore suitable for describing the tribal groups of the Huns. These *cunei* were fielded by both Roman *limitanei* and *comitatenses* armies. In *limitanei* armies, cavalry *vexillationes* could be called *alae* or *cunei*. It certainly seems plausible that while the Huns did not have a wedge-like formation resembling the deliberate Roman Army formation, their massed tribal cavalry groups may have looked like wedges of cavalry. The term is not glossed when used of the Huns so we can assume contemporaries understood what was meant – Ammianus does explain what the terms *barritus* (the war cry) and *clibanarii* (armoured cavalry) were.

There are other problems with Ammianus' description and it is clear that racial stereotypes are at play. The idea that Huns avoided forts and entrenchments (*Res gestae* 31.2.8) cannot be reconciled with the activities of the Huns in the 440s and 450s, although some scholars would still see the Huns as being incapable of assaulting cities. The taking of Naissus, Aquileia and other cities – even the breaching of the walls of Aurelianum

ABOVE LEFT
The Przewalski's horse breed, or Takhi, seems to share many similarities with the horses the Huns rode. Smaller in stature, stockier and with shorter legs than Arabian horses – typically 12–14 hands in height – they are also hardy and, while not fast (perhaps a factor in the race for the ridge crest at the battle of the Catalaunian Plains), they have good stamina. The short, upright mane of the Przewalski's horse accords with depictions of manes in Hunnic art. The tail is also shorter than that of other horse breeds and they have thicker hooves, which improve their performance across a variety of terrain types. (Joe Ravi/Wikimedia/ CC BY-SA 3.0)

ABOVE RIGHT
The winter coat of a Przewalski's horse. Maurice's *Strategikon* (Preface to Book 7) recommended attacking the Huns in February or March, when their horses would be in a wretched condition after suffering through the winter. (Lawrence/Wikimedia/CC BY 2.0)

– put such theories to bed, however. Nevertheless, Ammianus' description holds true for some Hunnic tactics right through to the age of Attila:

> in one respect you may pronounce them the most formidable of all warriors, for when at a distance they use missiles of various kinds tipped with sharpened bones instead of the usual points of javelins, and these bones are admirably fastened to the shaft of the javelin or arrow; but when they are at close quarters they fight with the sword, without any regard for their own safety; and often while their antagonists are warding off their blows they entangle them with twisted cords [*contortis laciniis iligant*], so that their hands being fettered, they lose all power of either riding or walking. (*Res gestae* 31.2.9)

Zosimus (*Nea Historia* 4.20.4) mentions Hunnic tactics: wheeling, charging, retreating in good time and shooting from their horses. This picture is confirmed by Sidonius, although in somewhat poetic terms; he tells us (*Carmina* 2.262–70) that Hun children were born for battles, and scarcely had they learned to stand, they were put on the back of a horse. Even Jerome, in a letter to Heliodorus in 396, lamented that the Roman Army, once victor and lord of the world, now trembled with terror 'at the sight of the foe and accepts defeat from men who cannot walk afoot and fancy themselves dead once they are unhorsed' (*Letters* 60.17).

Sidonius gives us some more detail in his panegyric on the Western Roman emperor Anthemius (r. 267–72); Anthemius was appointed *comes rei militaris* in 453 to rebuild the Danubian frontier after Attila's death. Sidonius describes (*Carmina* 2.243–75) the Huns as being at one with their horses. He also gives insight into Hunnic tactics (*Carmina* 2.266–69): they delighted in shapely bows and arrows and were supremely confident in their skill to hit their mark, and that they never missed.

Roman

In many ways the tactics of the Roman cavalry appear to have remained unchanged since the 4th century, despite their failings at Adrianople in 378. Making up between one-fifth and one-third of *limitanei* and *comitatenses* armies, cavalry units still consisted largely of medium cavalry, armoured in mail or scale, with round shields, and armed with swords and thrusting spears. Heavily armoured *clibanarii* and *cataphractii*, armed with the two-handed lance (*kontos*) are, however, still represented by shield designs in the *Notitia Dignitatum*. Vegetius tells us (*De Re Militari* 1.20 & 3.26) that there had been great progress in the realm of horsemanship within the Roman Empire thanks to the influence of the Goths, Alans and Huns. This was probably reflected in the presence of units of horse-archers and mounted missile units. These units were usually deployed on the wings in support of infantry units, although in the campaigns against Attila – especially at the battles of the Utus and the Catalaunian Plains – they seem to have played a more major role.

Another, later, treatise is also surprisingly useful for military concerns about the Huns. The *Strategikon*, which has come down to us under the name of the emperor Maurice, is one of the most important Byzantine military treatises. Probably written between 575 and 628, the work incorporates earlier material on the Huns and how their tactics could be countered. At the time the *Strategikon* was written the Huns themselves had ceased to be a threat although the treatise addresses 'Hunnic peoples', so those who fought in the same ways as the Huns under Attila had and other branches of Huns further east with whom the Byzantine Empire still came into contact.

The *Strategikon* is intended as a practical handbook and is addressed to the commander of an army. The commander is encouraged (Preface to Book 7) to make war against the Huns in February or March, when their horses would be in a wretched condition after suffering through the winter. This may have

This detail from a late-4th-century mosaic from Antioch depicting an Amazonomachy (a mythical battle between the ancient Greeks and the Amazons), now in the Louvre, Paris, shows Late Roman horse trappings and furniture. Although the male figure wears a muscled cuirass, he carries a Late Roman cavalry shield. We still find muscled cuirasses depicted on consular diptychs and elsewhere, so it is possible they were still worn by officers. (Carole Raddato/ Wikimedia/CC BY-SA 2.0)

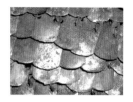

An example of Roman scale armour (*lorica squamata*), now in the Somerset County Museum in Taunton, England. Several pieces of Late Roman scale armour have been found at various sites although the design remained unchanged for centuries. The two most common armours were scale (*squamata*) and mail or chainmail (*hamata*). (Gaius Cornelius/Wikimedia/Public Domain)

been a misunderstanding of the thicker coat that Takhi horses grow in winter. Maurice also suggests waging open battle against the Huns, forcing them into close hand-to-hand fighting – precisely the kind of fighting that characterized the battles of the Utus and the Catalaunian Plains; the former hand-to-hand, the latter open battle (Jordanes, *Getica* 192). Maurice also recommends raids against the Huns if they make camp without precautions (perhaps this was what Arnegisclus was attempting at the battle of the Utus). If the Huns are reckless and impetuous, Roman delay is advised; fight them late in the day when their ardour has cooled. According to Jordanes (*Getica* 196), the battle of the Catalaunian Plains began only at the ninth hour (1500hrs); this might suggest the following of such advice.

In Book 11 of the *Strategikon*, an entire section is devoted to dealing with the Hunnish peoples – Avars, Turks and others – and much of what Maurice says is similar to the comments on the Xiongnu recorded in Chinese sources. Maurice tells us that the Huns were armed with mail, swords, bows and lances. Most attacked double-armed, that is with bow and lance slung, making use of either as required. Special attention is given to archery from horseback. The horses of the Huns' important men are likewise armoured. Maurice's intention in these descriptions was to familiarize Byzantine commanders with the foes they faced so they would know what to expect. He explains (*Strategikon* 11.2) that the Hunnish battle line is not made in three parts as the Roman battle line was (and this is precisely how the Roman battle line at the Catalaunian Plains is described). Instead, several units of irregular size join together to suggest a single Hunnish battle line. This suggests that the different tribal groups would remain independent of one another on the battlefield and fight as such. Spare horses were kept behind the battle line. Battle waged at a distance was preferred by the Huns, according to Maurice, using ambushes, the encirclement of enemies, simulated retreats and sudden returns, in scattered groups, and with wedge-shaped formations. This last point seems to tie Maurice's description into Ammianus' description of Hun tactics from more than a century earlier. We should note, however, that at the Utus and the Catalaunian Plains, these types of encounters were (deliberately?) avoided. Likewise, Maurice's notes on Hunnish weaknesses also echo earlier descriptions: he points out that the Hunnish peoples are hurt by a shortage of fodder for their horses and that when fighting infantry in close formation they do not dismount, as they do not last long fighting on foot having been raised on horseback.

To counter the Huns, Maurice recommends (*Strategikon* 11.2) fighting on level, unobstructed ground; Roman cavalry should advance against them in a single dense mass and engage in hand-to-hand fighting – just as took place at the Catalaunian Plains. Night attacks are also recommended; the account of the aftermath of the Catalaunian Plains suggests that night attacks were attempted by both Thorismund and Aëtius, but Thorismund was wounded and Aëtius got lost. Maurice recommends that infantry should be in the front line against the Huns, with cavalry deployed behind the Roman infantry; a deployment not followed at the Catalaunian Plains.

Several of these recommendations seem to match Roman tactics attempted during the battles of the 440s and 450s – hand-to-hand combat, perhaps a single charge at the Utus – but others were not, such as the Roman/allied use of the ridge at the Catalaunian Plains and the lack of infantry in the Roman/

This ivory diptych from Aosta Cathedral, Italy, depicts the consul Anicius Petronius Probus and the emperor Honorius. Dating from the early 5th century, it shows elaborate muscled cuirasses and two different designs of *spatha*. On the right, Probus is shown with a dished round shield with central handgrip. (DEA PICTURE LIBRARY/Getty Images)

allied front lines. The tactic of feigned flight is also addressed by Maurice and this too leads us to reconsider the battle of the Catalaunian Plains. As a defence against the feigned retreat, Maurice recommends (*Strategikon* 2.1) that the army should be drawn up in two lines. At the Catalaunian Plains, when Thorismund and Aëtius moved to the ridge crest with the Alans behind them, they did precisely this: if they pursued and the Hun retreat was feigned, the second Roman/allied line could help repel the renewed Hunnic charge. Maurice also warned (*Strategikon* 11.2) not to be too hasty in pursuing retreating Huns; this caution might also have characterized Roman/allied operations against the Huns (though not, it seems, by Thorismund). Maurice advises, however, that pursuing troops should not fall more than three or four bowshots behind the enemy.

Another recommendation made by Maurice (*Strategikon* 7.2.2) is that, against archers, a general should not draw up his battle line on the lower slopes, but instead form up on higher ground. Alternatively, he should attempt to fight on level ground. Maurice advises (*Strategikon* 7.2.17) that cavalry should be drilled in manoeuvring over hilly, thick and rough ground and trained to ascend and descend quickly on sloping terrain. It seems clear from Jordanes' account of the battle of the Catalaunian Plains, with the race for the ridge crest, that these recommended methods have much in common with the tactics actually employed by Aëtius and Theodoric I.

Naissus

AD 443

BACKGROUND TO BATTLE

A contingent of Huns was present in the Gothic armies of the 370s and the Huns themselves made incursions across the Danube into Pannonia in the immediate aftermath of the battle of Adrianople in 378. More crossings were to come in 381/82, 383/84 and 386, although most sources are again silent on the specifics of who the enemy was. Ambrose, bishop of Mediolanum, mentions (*Letters* 24.8) the threat posed to Italy by Huns and Alans operating in the provinces of Raetia and Noricum in a letter to the Western Roman emperor Valentinian II (r. 375–92), dating from 383 or possibly 387. The Huns may have been employed as *foederati* by Roman armies in the 380s and 390s in both the West and East (Ambrose, *Letters* 24.8; Pacatus, *Speeches* 32.4–5; John of Antioch, *Historia chronike* F187).

A *solidus* of the Western Roman emperor Valentinian III, struck *c.*430–55. (Classical Numismatic Group/Wikimedia/ CC BY-SA 2.5)

The first large-scale raids by the Huns as a whole people began in 395, attacking across the Don River into the Caucasus Mountains and Persia and the Roman provinces south and south-west of Armenia. Jerome tells us (*Letters* 60.16 & 77.8) that these raids were prompted by famine; the Huns took cattle, but they also captured thousands of slaves. One branch of this invasion reached the Persian capital Ctesiphon, another branch was defeated after crossing the Euphrates River, and a third ravaged Asia Minor and Syria. Another invasion crossed into Thrace and threatened the Roman province of Dalmatia. Modern opinion remains

Of Alanic-Gothic descent, Flavius Ardabur Aspar was an important *magister militum* of Eastern Roman Empire armies. His son Ardabur (shown here with his father in 434) served with him. Aspar was an important commander in the East and played a crucial role in the defeat of the usurper Iohannes in the West, as well as in the accession of the emperor Marcian (r. 450–57). Only Priscus (*History* F9.4/61) and Marcellinus Comes (*Chronicle* 441) suggest that Aspar faced Attila, despite the two leaders being exact contemporaries. Aspar had been *magister militum* since 431, when he commanded the Eastern Roman Empire fleet. Marcellinus Comes states (*Chronicle* 441) that Aspar and Anatolius, both *magistri militum*, made peace with Attila in 441. Aspar seems to have been of Alanic-Gothic origin and shared a Gothic descent with his fellow commanders. Arnegisclus was probably of Gothic heritage; his son Anagast, who would also fight the Huns, also bore a Gothic name. So too Areobindus. Thus, we can see how the descendants of the Gothic invaders of the 4th century had become vital to the military command structure of the armies of both halves of the Roman Empire. Various shields are depicted at the bottom of this *missorium*, even a rectangular *scutum* of a style that was no longer used. (Sailko/Wikimedia/CC BY 2.5)

divided as to whether these invasions were coordinated or not, but they lasted until 398.

In 406, the Hunnic leader Uldin, who seems to have controlled the northern Danube shore, made an alliance with the Roman general Stilicho (Jordanes, *Romana* 321), but in 408 invaded and ravaged across the Danube, taking advantage of the death of the Eastern emperor Arcadius (r. 383–408) and the fall of Stilicho (Sozomen, *Ecclesiastical History* 9.5.2–7). This was a pattern of relations that would be repeated down to the time of Attila.

We are notably uninformed on the history of the Huns in the 410s and 420s, mainly due to the loss of Olympiodorus' work, but Marcellinus Comes announces (*Chronicle* 422) that the Huns devastated Thrace in 422. This event may have been taken seriously by the Romans, as in that same year, Theodosius II issued an edict (*Theodosian Code* 7.8.13) specifying that the garrison at Constantinople was to be accommodated so as to be ready to react quickly to any threat. This, however, is the only mention in all the surviving sources of the period. In the West, however, Hun troops were fighting for the usurper Iohannes, which suggests they had been enrolled into the Roman Army by that point. As a child, Aëtius was a hostage of the Hunnic king Uldin and then his successor Charaton (Olympiodorus, *Gle Syggrathes* F19). In 423 he joined Iohannes' court and was sent to secure a Hunnic army to help Iohannes fight off the ambitions of Theodosius II, who wanted to install his six-year-old nephew Valentinian as emperor of the Western Roman Empire. When Aëtius returned with the Hunnic army in 425 (having purchased their assistance with a large sum of gold), Iohannes had already been defeated and Aëtius used his army to secure his new position in relation to Valentinian III, the newly proclaimed emperor (r. 425–55) of the Western Roman Empire and his court, especially Valentinian III's mother, Galla Placidia. These events are recorded by Gregory of Tours (*Historia Francorum* 2.8); Gregory records the account of the (otherwise lost) *Historia* of Renatus Profuturus Frigiderius concerning Aëtius. Aëtius moved on to a command in Gaul and whatever agreement the Romans had reached with the Huns was soon broken. In 427 the Huns who had settled in Pannonia were attacked and conquered (Marcellinus Comes, *Chronicles* 427; Jordanes, *Getica* 166).

By 430 two new kings of the Huns had emerged, the brothers Octar – or Uptaros (Socrates, *Ecclesiastical History* 7.30) – and Ruga, also named as Rua, Ruas (Jordanes, *Getica* 180) and Rugila (*Chronicle of 511*). They ruled different territories, so neither was the *regon protos*. Octar and Ruga had another brother, Mundzuc, also known as Mundiucus, Moundioukhos and Moundiou. Mundzuc had two sons, Bleda and Attila. Many have seen Octar and Ruga as dual kings, although we are clearly told they ruled different sections of the Huns. Octar died in 430 and was probably succeeded by his eldest nephew, Bleda.

Under Ruga, peace was again made by Aëtius with the Roman Empire (Prosper, *Epitoma Chronicon* a.432). In 434 or 435 Ruga died (*Gallic Chronicle of 452* a.434; Theodoret, *Ecclesiastical History* 5.37.4) and Attila became king with his brother Bleda, even if Bleda ruled over the majority of Hunnic territory (Jordanes, *Getica* 181; Prosper, *Epitoma Chronicon* a.451; Priscus, *History* F2). Just prior to his death, Ruga had secured the payment of a tribute to maintain a peace established with the Eastern Roman Empire; there seems to have been some fighting prior to that. The tribute had been 350lb of gold per year and was now doubled to 700lb (Priscus, *History* F2), but it would remain unpaid. Having concluded peace with the Romans, Bleda and Attila marched their forces against the Sorgosi (Priscus, *History* F2), an otherwise unknown people, but the campaign may actually have been against the Sassanid Persians. It appears to have been unsuccessful, although our knowledge is very minimal.

In 440 a large fleet had left Vandal-held Carthage and landed in Sicily. The Vandal king, Gaiseric (r. 428–77), had captured Carthage the year before and now threatened the central Mediterranean. Gaiseric overran parts of western Sicily before returning to Carthage. In response to this crisis, Valentinian III proclaimed that Theodosius II (his uncle) would send an army to deal with the crisis. Commanded by Areobindus and several other commanders, the predominantly Gothic army landed in Sicily in 441 after Gaiseric's departure, but the troops were soon plundering the island themselves. Areobindus was still in Constantinople in March that year; it seems that the Huns launched their invasion as soon as he departed from Constantinople for Sicily – and, what is more, the Huns knew that the time was right to strike.

We are ill-informed about the campaigns of 441–43. It would seem, based on Priscus (*History* F1b, F2 & F3 – but the order of the fragments

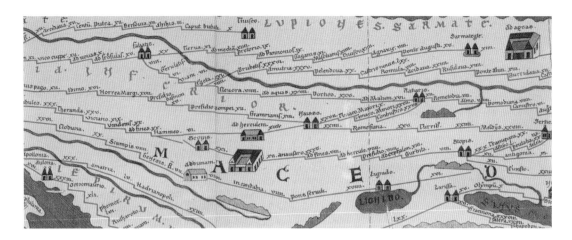

is F2, F3, F1b) that a huge campaign was launched by the Huns in 441. Priscus writes (*History* F2) of a fort (*phroyrion*) being taken at the time of the annual fair held in Margus (modern-day Požarevac, Serbia), opposite the site of the fort of Constantia. This can be dated to the beginning of the campaign in 441. Priscus subsequently writes (*History* F3) of 'some forts' (*phroyria tina*), so this fragment relates to later events. It is possible that the Huns crossed at Viminacium (near modern-day Kostolac and Požarevac, Serbia) as well (Procopius, *On Buildings* 4.5.12–13). Marcellinus Comes suggests (*Chronicle* 441) a more complete picture, however, despite placing all the events in 441. For the year 441, he records that the Huns plundered the lands of the Romans after which peace was made with Attila for one year. The Huns subsequently complained that the peace terms had not been met, however, and invaded again in 443.

If we combine our accounts, and shift Marcellinus Comes' account of events from 441 to 442–43 (and assume a year-long truce), they correspond to the other evidence we have (*Chronicon Paschale* Olympiad 305, 442; Prosper, *Epitoma Chronicon* a.442). This version of events suggests that there was a campaign in 441, peace for a year in 442, and then a renewed campaign in 443. What is more, Prosper tells us (*Epitoma Chronicon* a.442) that the army that should have defended the Danube was in Sicily, diverted there for a war with the Vandals. This implies that Attila's raid that year (441 not 442), with its devastating success and meeting seemingly little resistance, may have been carefully planned and perhaps mounted in the light of knowledge that the Roman forces would be absent. Procopius states (*On Buildings* 4.5.6) that Attila invaded in 441 with a great army and razed fortresses with no difficulty; and no one stood against him. Procopius goes on to tells us (*On Buildings* 4.5.12–13) that Singidunum (modern-day Belgrade, Serbia) was captured by the 'barbarians' and razed; Viminacium was also ruined and later restored by the Eastern Roman emperor Justinian I. These two centres, both important cities on the *via militaris* ('military road'), were probably sacked by the Huns in 441. If armies to defend the Roman Empire were not present, however, it is understandable that peace was made and tribute paid. This entailed the payment of 6,000lb of gold and a further 1,000lb per year – an increase from the 700lb agreed in 435.

The importance of Naissus can be seen in this detail from the *Tabula Peutingeriana* (Peutinger Map), a 13th-century parchment copy of an original Roman road map now in the Austrian National Library (Österreichischse Nationalbibliotek), Vienna. In the detail, it can be seen that Naissus is located at the intersection of several roads and the fact that it and Ratiaria were targeted by the Huns reveals a deliberate strategy. (Konrad Miller/ Wikimedia/Public Domain)

MAP KEY

1 The Huns cross the Danube into the province of Dacia Ripensis in late spring 443. They take Ratiaria before moving south-west towards Naissus on the Nišava River in the province of Dacia Mediterranea. Circling around the city, the Huns cross the Nišava south of the city.

2 The garrison of Naissus stays behind the walls of the city and does not venture out to prevent the crossing or thwart the preparations for the coming siege, perhaps expecting that the Huns would not attempt (or be able) to take the city.

3 The Huns have made meticulous preparations for a siege and bring the materials required for their siege machines: archery beams and rams. They surround the city and clear the ramparts of defenders with archery fire from their beams.

4 The Huns bring up rams to the city walls. The defenders are able to destroy some Hunnic rams with chunks of masonry and hurled stones.

5 The walls are breached with rams and ladders and the Huns pour into the city. The destruction of the city is total; it remains a ruin and is unoccupied five years later.

Battlefield environment

The first Roman city that Attila and his Huns targeted in 443 was Naissus (modern-day Niš, Serbia) on the Nišava River. Naissus had long been a focus of barbarian invasions stretching back to the 3rd century. The city was an important one in the province of Dacia Mediterranea and the seat of a subordinate bishop within the diocese of Dacia. It was also the birthplace of the emperor Constantine I (r. 306–37). Naissus controlled land access to the Balkans, Greece and Thrace. It lay upon the *via militaris*, the 'military road' from Singidunum (modern-day Belgrade, Serbia) on the Danube, down the Morava River to Constantinople. The road passed through a series of important fortified cities such as Viminacium (near modern-day Kostolac and Požarevac, Serbia), and then, after Naissus, Serdica (modern-day Sofia, Bulgaria),

Philippopolis (modern-day Plovdiv, Bulgaria), Adrianople (modern-day Edirne, Turkey) and Constantinople. This 8m-wide road, first built in the 1st century AD, would offer armies a convenient route of invasion down to the 14th century. It was also the meeting point of four additional roads and controlled two river valleys. Control of Naissus was therefore vital and the Hunnic attack on it was especially calculated – a fact borne out by the preparations evident in Priscus' account and the deliberate (and seemingly painstaking) destruction. By choosing to make an example of Naissus for such attention, the Huns could send a message in all directions of what other centres could expect and that, perhaps contrary to expectations, city walls no longer provided a safe refuge.

This panoramic view of Niš shows the importance of the Nišava River to the city. The Ottoman fortress can be seen on the far bank; it contains Roman ruins, which will have been those ravaged by Attila's forces. Priscus describes (*History* F1b/6.2) how the Huns bridged the river where it flows past the city to the south, allowing a large number of Huns to cross easily. (Aleksic Ivan/Wikimedia/CC BY-SA 3.0)

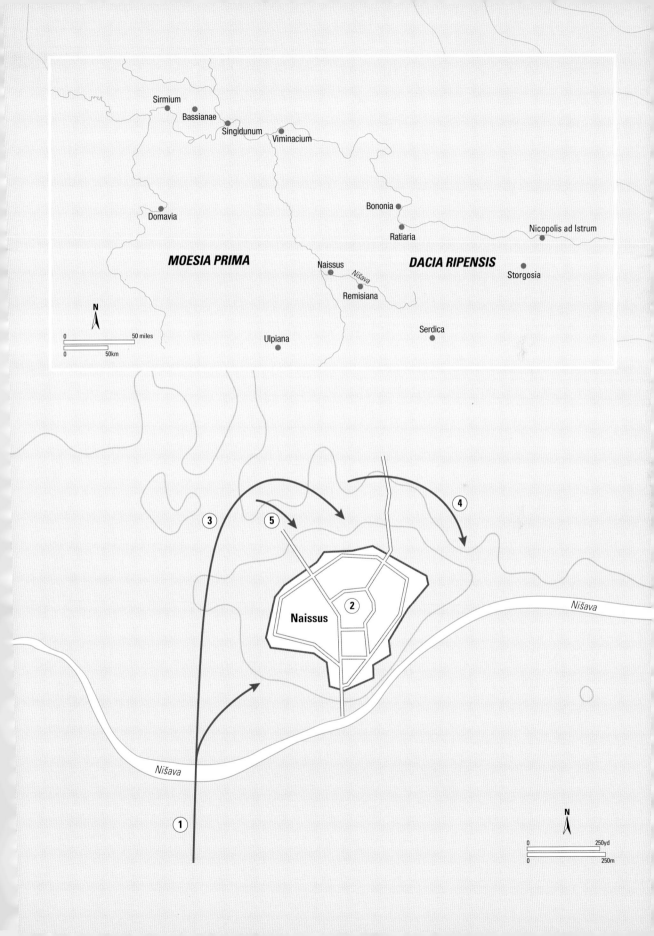

Sirmium

Bassianae

Singidunum

Viminacium

Bononia

Ratiaria

Nicopolis ad Istrum

Domavia

MOESIA PRIMA

Naissus

Nišava

DACIA RIPENSIS

Storgosia

Remisiana

Serdica

Ulpiana

N

0   50 miles

0   50km

Nišava

Naissus

Nišava

N

0   250yd

0   250m

INTO COMBAT

After the campaign of 441 and the peace that followed in 442, the increased tribute remained unpaid. In 443, having still not received the outstanding tribute, the Huns renewed hostilities; the wide-ranging devastation of Illyricum and Thrace that then took place convinced Theodosius II to pay the tribute. Attila and his brother Bleda probably crossed into Roman territory at Ratiaria (modern-day Arcear, Bulgaria) in Dacia Ripensis in late spring 443. They quickly moved on to Naissus, located on the Nišava River in the province of Dacia Mediterranea. Naissus was not only an important city in its province, it was also the point where five roads met, making it a central node of transport and communication. These roads led to Lissus (modern-day Lezhë, Albania) via Scupi (modern-day Skopje, North Macedonia) to the south-west, Serdica (modern-day Sofia, Bulgaria) to the east (along the *via militaris*), Singidunum to the north-west, Thessaloniki (modern-day Thessalonica, Greece) to the south, and Ratiaria to the north-east. For the Huns, taking Naissus would allow rapid access to any of the other Roman road stations along those roads and, using the *via militaris*, swift access to Constantinople itself. Naissus and Ratiaria were also the locations of arms factories (*fabricae*) manned by military personnel, and would therefore have had a military presence, even though Naissus was not on the border with the Roman Empire as Dacia Ripensis was. Its garrison will have been small, however, most probably consisting of units or vexillations from the *limitaneus* of Dacia Ripensis or other units from the *comitatus* of Thrace and perhaps some men who had fled from Ratiaria; it is unclear whether Ratiaria was also besieged by the Huns, but it is highly probable.

A relatively long fragment of Priscus (*History* F1b/6.2) gives us the details of the fall of Naissus. Priscus begins by telling us of the city's history, founded by Constantine (this is incorrect – Naissus was Constantine I's birthplace). Somewhat problematically, the fragment as preserved by Constantine VII Porphyrogenitus states that the city was on the *Danouba* river; Naissus is nowhere near the Danube River, however, lying as it does on the Nišava River. Priscus also uses the word *Danouba*, but he uses the term *Istros* for the Danube; we do not know the ancient name for the Nišava.

The imperial villa of Mediana in Naissus (now in the eastern suburbs of modern-day Niš, Serbia) was the victim of the Hunnic siege in 443. Dating from the reign of the emperor Constantine I (r. 306–37), it was his place of birth in *c.*272 and later used by the emperors Constans (r. 337–50), Constantius II (r. 337–61) and Julian (r. 361–63). The villa was undoubtedly plundered by the Huns during their assault on the city. (Marcin Szala/Wikimedia/CC BY-SA 3.0)

Priscus states briefly (*History* F1b/6.2) that the Huns approached Naissus with every intention to take the well-populated and well-fortified city. The defenders inside the city did not venture out; Priscus admonishes them (*History* F1b/6.2) for lacking the courage to offer battle. This, however, may have reflected an accepted policy, undertaken in the expectation that the Huns would not attack cities – or at least be unsuccessful if they did so. The attitude found in Ammianus (*Res gestae* 31.2.8) that barbarians and 'savages' did not attack cities may still have held in 443, but the fate of Naissus would show the Romans that even cities were not safe. The harsh treatment of Naissus by the Huns may have been meted out specifically to drive that point home – the city was located some way from the border, had a small garrison and may have been punished to send the message that no city was safe.

Priscus tells us (*History* F1b/6.2) that the Huns bridged the Nišava where it flows past the city to the south and that a large number of Huns were able to cross easily. Siege engines were then brought up to the walls. This

This mosaic from the Basilica of Santa Maria Maggiore, Rome, shows a city besieged by troops. Note the mix of shield designs (both round and oval) and that some soldiers seem not to be wearing armour. Decorated tunics can be seen in the lower panel. (DEA/G. NIMATALLAH/Getty Images)

implies that the Hun intention to take the city was deliberate and that they had taken the time to make preparations for a siege and/or to find allies who were experienced in such operations. Some modern-day commentators, notably Thompson, doubt the Hunnic capacity to mount a siege and they accuse Priscus of wholesale invention. It is entirely possible, however, that the Huns were assisted by engineers who had been captured or had offered their services to the invaders. The interactions of Huns with the Roman world during the first decades of the 5th century would have allowed men to learn such skills, perhaps in Roman service. Because Attila and the Huns were unable to take Aurelianum in 451 – and ignoring the successful Hunnic investment of Aquileia (near modern-day Trieste, Italy), Mediolanum (modern-day Milan, Italy) and Ticinum (modern-day Pavia, Italy) in 452 – some historians have seen accounts of the successful taking of Naissus and the complex siege machinery Attila brought to bear as being unlikely. On the other hand, taking such a city would prompt others to submit and pay tribute, which is exactly what they did. It should also be borne in mind that the defences of Aurelianum and the Roman cities besieged in 452 were also far more substantial than those of Naissus; they were even especially prepared to withstand the Huns (Jordanes, *Getica* 195) but they fell all the same.

Priscus took notes on his journey, but Thompson (1996: 16) indicts his lack of competence as a military historian. One reason for modern-day commentators' doubts about Priscus' account of the siege of Naissus is his echoing of classical authors – his language is reminiscent of the 5th- and 4th-century BC Greek writers Herodotus, Thucydides and Xenophon, and also that of Dexippus, writing in the 3rd century AD but modelling himself on Thucydides. Their accounts contain the sieges of Plataea (near modern-day Plataies, Greece) in 431–427 BC and of Philippopolis (modern-day Plovdiv, Bulgaria) in AD 250, in Dexippus especially. What Priscus describes at Naissus, however, differs from the accounts given by those authors – despite some verbal and stylistic echoing – and we can probably trust in Priscus'

account more than some historians have done. Thompson (1996: 13) rejected it out of hand, however. In Thompson's view, the verbal echoes were instead intended to shore up Priscus' judgement of the significance of the siege, which he considers one of the worst to befall Rome.

As described in the sources, the nature of the Hunnic siege weapons was relatively uncomplicated and in some respects unique; it is possible that they were a Hunnic invention, thereby accounting for their subsequent ineffectiveness against stronger defences – although there is evidence too that they remained highly effective. Priscus describes (*History* F1b/6.2) beams laid on wheels; on these were mounted plaited-willow and rawhide screens to protect the archers standing on the beams who shot arrows at the defenders on the ramparts. The screens protected the archers from the defenders' missiles and incendiary devices. Men stationed at the ends of the beams pushed them forward on their wheels to where they were needed. Priscus relates (*History* F1b/6.2) that many such devices were constructed, and that the sheer number of projectiles fired by the Huns made the defenders on the ramparts withdraw. Once this was achieved, rams were brought up to the city walls. According to Priscus (*History* F1b/6.2), the rams were constructed of beams inclining towards one another, with loose chains hanging down onto which a beam was fastened (something like an A-frame). Similar to the archery beams, the rams had protective screens to stop incendiary and missile attacks from harming the operators. Priscus also writes (*History* F1b/6.2) of protective spearheads – perhaps to provide extra protection should the defenders launch an infantry

Roman ruins inside the grounds of the Niš Fortress. These Roman foundations were clearly built upon subsequently. The town of Naissus was partially rebuilt by the Eastern Roman emperor Justinian I (r. 527–65), but the city never fully recovered from the devastation wrought by the Huns. (Novak Watchmen/Wikimedia/Public Domain)

assault against the rams. From behind the protective screens, men would draw back the beam on its loose chains using cords and then let it swing towards a pre-arranged spot on the wall. This technique would cause a part of the wall to 'collapse and disappear' (Priscus F1b/6.2). Syvänne (2020: 84–86) includes some speculative reconstructions of the siege machines, although he dates the siege to 441.

Despite Priscus' criticism of the defenders, they were not passively waiting for the walls to come down. He relates (*History* F1b/6.2) that the Romans threw stones, some as big as wagons (presumably chunks of masonry), from the walls at the rams. Fields (2015: 27) translates this as wagon loads of stone, but both Blockley (1983: 233) and Given (2014: 15) prefer 'wagon-sized' stones. One of these attacks reportedly crushed a Hun ram complete with its crew (Priscus, *History* F1b/F6.2). Despite their best efforts, the defenders were no match for the number of rams eventually brought against the walls. This detail (Priscus, *History* F1b/6.2), and the number of arrows fired, suggest that the large number of Huns brought against the city outnumbered the small Roman garrison many times over. The Huns also brought up ladders and assaulted the walls in combination with the rams and archers. We do not hear of the utilization of the *fabrica* for the defence of the city, or indeed of it being destroyed or sabotaged in anticipation of the Hunnic victory. We can probably assume, therefore, that by targeting both Ratiaria and Naissus, the Huns sought to arm themselves with Roman arms and equipment; Naissus, however, was afforded special punishment.

The walls were breached by the rams and Hunnic warriors mounted ladders to take the adjacent walls. The attackers poured in and soon opened up Naissus for the Hunnic cavalry, who charged into the city, plundering and slaughtering. Very few of the city's inhabitants escaped, although they may have made their way to the north, towards Ratiaria – but there was no guaranteed safety there, given that the Huns were moving in that direction. It is possible that some troops and refugees escaped to Serdica, although that city too would soon fall victim to the Huns. The Huns plundered Naissus with extreme brutality and destroyed its walls; in 447 Naissus would be bypassed by Huns once again on the rampage, implying that it was still in ruins and not worth troubling over, had nothing left to take, or both.

In 448 Priscus travelled to meet Attila on an embassy with Maximus and Bigilas (*History* F11.2/8.13–14). Upon passing Naissus, the Roman diplomats found that the city was still all but deserted; only some diseased people (perhaps lepers) were living in the ruins. Priscus and his companions were forced to camp upstream from the city because the banks of the river were still covered in the bones of the dead. This might imply a battle outside the walls, a massacre of refugees or perhaps just that the bodies inside the city had been removed but that there were not enough people left alive to bury them properly. The idea of bones being visible years after a defeat also recalled the battle of Adrianople (Ammianus, *Res gestae* 31.7.16), and before that, the Varian disaster in AD 9: Germanicus Caesar (the adopted son of the emperor Tiberius) came across the bones of the massacred legions of Varus six years later in AD 15 (Tacitus, *Annales* 1.61). We might therefore suspect Priscus' detail of discovering the bones as being an exaggeration,

but he paints the loss of Naissus as a disaster of similarly grave proportions – and no one who knew their Roman history would fail to notice the comparison made between the fate of Naissus and that of Adrianople and the Varian disaster.

Serdica, further east along the *via militaris*, was also ravaged by the Huns in 443, although it and Ratiaria remained functioning cities afterwards. This suggests that Naissus was indeed singled out early in the campaign for the harshest-possible treatment as an example of Hun capability. It is even possible that the Huns allowed refugees to escape from Naissus to facilitate the spread of news and panic concerning the Hunnic threat. We know from Nestorius' *Bazaar of Heracleides*, written in *c.*451 and in the relative safety of Egypt, that the threat posed by Attila's united Huns was widely appreciated by the Romans.

Excavations of buried silverware, perhaps hidden as the Huns approached or sacked Naissus in 443, hint at the fear felt by the Romans in the face of the Hunnic threat. A set of five silver plates celebrating the tenth anniversary of the emperor Licinius I (r. 308–24), and therefore dating from 318, were found in Niš in 1901. It is possible that these were buried during the Gothic Wars of the later 4th century, although the siege by the Huns was the greatest danger Naissus had ever faced and makes the Hunnic assault on the city a more likely context. A bronze head of the emperor Constantine I was found in one of the riverbanks of the Nišava during bridge construction in 1900; its presence may be another sign of Hunnic depredations.

Durostorum (modern-day Silistra, Bulgaria), the birthplace of Flavius Aëtius in the 390s, was not immune to the ravages of the Huns. It became an important military base on the Danube in the 4th century and in the 5th century saw further strengthening of its walls, perhaps partly in response to Hunnic successes against cities such as Naissus. (Svik/ Wikimedia/CC BY-SA 3.0)

The Utus River

AD 447

BACKGROUND TO BATTLE

As his remorseless advance of 443 continued eastwards along the *via militaris*, Attila advanced on Constantinople itself, probably putting it under siege, but he could not breach the city's walls. Instead, he turned south and ravaged the Gallipoli peninsula, taking Callipolis (modern-day Gelibolu, Turkey) and Sestus (near modern-day Eceabat, Turkey). A Roman army was defeated at Callipolis although we have no further details. A fragment of Priscus (*History* F9.4/61) suggests that armies commanded by Flavius Ardabur Aspar, Flavius Areobindus and Arnegisclus – the last of whom was also known as Arnigisclus, Argagisclus and Anargiscus; Priscus also calls him Ornigisklos (*History* F38) – were badly defeated in more than one battle before a large number of Roman cities were ravaged. All three commanders were of Gothic descent. Priscus tells us (*History* F38) that Aspar was sent back from Sicily with the army dispatched there with Areobindus and Arnegisclus to deal with the Vandal threat. Aspar had arranged the truce in 442, a detail missing from Priscus; it comes from Marcellinus Comes (*Chronicle* 441). All three of these men were *magistri militum* and the most experienced commanders available to Theodosius II. Some commentators date this Priscus fragment (preserved in the *Chronographia* of Theophanes) to 447 rather than 443. Priscus states (*History* F38) that the Huns had overrun Ratiaria, Naissus, Philippopolis, Arcadiaopolis (modern-day Lüleburgaz, Turkey) and Constantia, plus other towns. The devastation could have included the destruction of Nicopolis ad Istrum (modern-day Nikyup, Bulgaria), but this might have occurred in 441. This path of destruction runs west to east, although 'Constantia' is probably the fortress opposite Margus.

Portrait bust of Theodosius II, now in the Louvre, Paris. The new walls of Constantinople built during his reign withstood the Hunnic siege of 443, but his tenure also saw the military disasters of the 440s in which the cities of Thrace were overrun and several Roman armies were destroyed. (Jastrow/ Wikimedia/CC BY-SA 2.5)

Priscus states (*History* F9.4/61) that the three generals were badly defeated and that Attila advanced on both seas (the Black Sea and the Sea of Marmara) at Callipolis and Sestus, and took every fortress except Adrianople (modern-day Edirne, Turkey) and Heracleia (Perinthus, near modern-day Mamara Ereğlisi, Turkey). The optimal timeframe for this rampage is the year 443, but Priscus may have conflated it with events in 447. Attila even reached the fortress of Athyras (near modern-day Büyükçekmece, Turkey), coming within 30km of Constantinople itself. Theodosius II was forced to make peace and to pay 6,000lb of gold as a lump sum to ensure Attila left Roman territory. Priscus here may have combined several campaigns in one; the siege of Constantinople, which led to the massive gold payment, probably came in 443. What is more, the appointment of three experienced generals to deal with Attila in 443 is of interest because they were unsuccessful and were all defeated. Arnegisclus would continue in his role as an army commander and meet his death at the Utus in 447. The author of the *Chronicon Paschale* states

(Olympiad 306, 447) that Ardabur was consul in that year too and so should have been responsible for some of the military defence.

One noteworthy aspect of the renewed Hun campaign in 443 is that, at its conclusion, the Huns secured the lump-sum payment of 6,000lb of gold. This was a huge amount and, usually, the Huns demanded a yearly tribute (it would be nearly 1,000lb per year going forward). What this may mean is that in 441, war was initiated by the Huns to secure the yearly tribute that had been promised in 435 at the Peace of Margus but had remained unpaid. The date of the earlier agreement is significant (see Thompson 1996: 267–68 & 271–72). It would seem that the invasion took place in 441 because the yearly tribute had not been paid and the fugitive exchange promised had not taken place either (Priscus, *History* F3). In 441, the Eastern Roman Empire was distracted by the Vandals (another reason for the Hun invasion) and was in no position to resist the Hunnic threat. Aspar and Anatolius therefore made peace for 442, perhaps promising that the tribute arrears would be paid. When the peace lapsed in 443 and the tribute still had not been paid, the Huns unleashed a wave of destruction that the Eastern Romans were still not prepared for, despite having had a year to make the necessary arrangements. Cities fell to the Huns, with Naissus providing the foremost example of what awaited other cities, and at the end of the campaign Theodosius II agreed to pay the tribute arrears in one lump sum. This would imply that the 6,000lb of gold amounted to eight or nine years of arrears, meaning the date of the Peace of Margus should be placed in 435/36 and not at an earlier or later date.

The Huns, having been paid their tribute, retired back over the Danube. The next event of importance was the death of Bleda and the emergence of Attila as sole king. In the sources, Bleda's death is often characterized as a murder carried out by Attila (Jordanes, *Getica* 181; Prosper, *Epitoma Chronicon* a.444; Marcellinus Comes, *Chronicle* 445). Regardless of the value of such assertions, we are unsure of the date of Bleda's death. There is some evidence in the sources that it could have occurred in 441, 444 (Prosper,

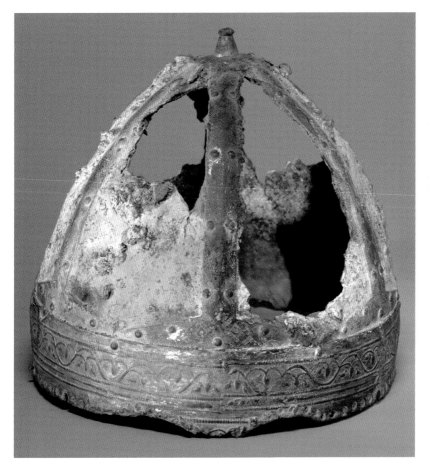

This 6th- or 7th-century *spangenhelm* is now in the Metropolitan Museum of Art, New York. The ridge helmet and the *spangenhelm* became ubiquitous and were used by all factions during the 4th and 5th centuries. Some are highly decorated, others plain, but all of those found show some degree of personalization; no two helmets are the same. (Metropolitan Museum of Art/ Wikimedia/CC0)

Epitoma Chronicon a.444), 445 (Marcellinus Comes, *Chronicle* 445) or 446 (*Gallic Chronicle of 452* a.446).

The *Gallic Chronicle of 452* informs us very briefly (a.445) that in 445 Thrace was shaken by an attack by the Huns; but no other source mentions an invasion in that year. For the year 447, however, we find that no fewer than 70 cities were laid waste by the Huns, and no assistance was forthcoming from the Western Roman Empire. Callinicus records (*Life of Saint Hypatius* 104) an even higher toll of devastation, stating that 100 cities were captured. Callinicus also claims that the population of Constantinople fled when the city was threatened. Callinicus makes no mention of the defeat at Utus for that year, but the destruction wrought by the Huns is evident.

In 447, Attila would lead his newly expanded armies into the Eastern Roman Empire province of Moesia Prima, perhaps crossing again at Ratiaria. This would be his first campaign as sole king. By this time, Theodosius II was well aware of the threat the Huns posed, the Roman forces having been defeated by them and the emperor having been forced to pay a massive indemnity in 443. Rather than pay again, and perhaps convinced that the Huns were weakened under a single king's rule, Theodosius II chose to oppose them militarily. Attila may have invaded because the yearly tributes of 1,000lb of gold had remained unpaid since 443; this would fit a familiar pattern although it is possible they were paid for at least a few years.

MAP KEY

1 Attila and the Huns have overrun large tracts of the Eastern Roman Empire in the late spring and summer of 447. Stopped at the pass of Thermopylae, they have turned back towards the Danube, laden with plunder.

2 The *magister utriusque militiae* Arnegisclus has led his forces from Marcianopolis to face the Hunnic threat. Arnegisclus pursues with his cavalry force (probably 8,000 men) and falls on the rear of the Hunnic column as they cross the Utus River.

3 Most of the Hunnic column is unable to turn and re-cross the Utus to fight the Romans, but Attila is able to lead a portion of the Hun force back across the river to shore up the rear of his column. Arnegisclus fights on even after he is unhorsed, but the Romans are outnumbered and eventually defeated.

4 After Arnegisclus is killed, the Roman survivors flee to Storgosia.

5 Attila continues his march to the Danube.

Battlefield environment

The Utus River (now the Vit River in Bulgaria), its original name derived from the Thracian word *utus* ('water'), flows for 188km in central and northern Bulgaria. It is a tributary of the Danube, rising in the Stara Planina (Balkan Mountains) and emptying into the Danube near Somovit, Bulgaria. The exact site of the battle along the river's length is not known. It makes most sense, however, that the battle was fought at the northern end of the river, nearer the Danube, since the Huns were returning to their homelands in 447 back across the Danube laden with plunder. Therefore, the battle was probably fought somewhere north of the fortified Roman road station of Storgosia (modern-day Pleven, Bulgaria), marked on the *Tabula Peutingeriana*, which may have provided a base for Arnegisclus' pursuit; Storgosia may even have been the closest road station to which the Roman survivors fled.

Other crossings of the Vit are located near the modern-day Bulgarian towns of Gulyantsi, Komarevo, Podem, Dolni Dabnik and Dolna Mitropoliya. We should perhaps search for a location where there was only a single crossing of the Utus and where the Huns who had already crossed could not return to assist the men at the end of their column. Such a single crossing might have meant that a smaller Roman contingent could have fought (on perhaps even terms) a portion of Hunnic forces. The location of a fortified road station close by would have also offered the Romans refuge if needed. This combination of factors would have given Arnegisclus the best chance of success.

The Vit in Gulyantsi, Bulgaria. Although we do not know exactly where on the Utus the battle was fought, there are only a few places where the river was fordable in antiquity. We should probably also seek a place where the Huns could not cross back over the river and encircle the outnumbered Romans. Nevertheless, Arnegisclus was overwhelmed and defeated. (Anton Lefterov/ Wikimedia/CC BY-SA 3.0)

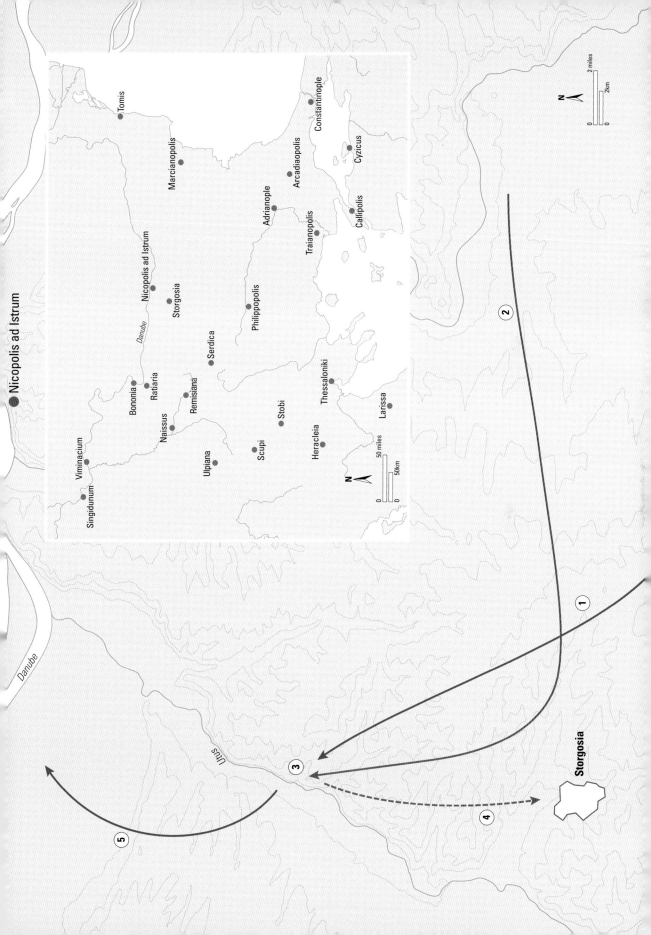

Nicopolis ad Istrum

Tomis

Marcianopolis

Constantinople

Cyzicus

Arcadiaopolis

Callipolis

Adrianople

Traianopolis

Nicopolis ad Istrum

Storgosia

Philippopolis

Danube

Serdica

Bononia

Ratiaria

Remisiana

Naissus

Stobi

Thessaloniki

Scupi

Heraclea

Larissa

Ulpiana

Viminacium

Singidunum

50 miles

50km

N

2 miles

2km

N

Danube

Utus

Storgosia

INTO COMBAT

Jordanes tells us (*Romana* 331) that Arnegisclus and the *comitatus* of Thrace marched from Marcianopolis (modern-day Devnya, Bulgaria) to face the Hunnic threat. It is possible that Arnegisclus chose to face Attila in direct contravention of orders to avoid a pitched battle; his co-commanders from 443, Aspar and Areobindus, are not mentioned in accounts of 447. Jordanes and Marcellinus Comes only call Arnegisclus *magister militum* (without giving any additional information about which command he held) and *dux* of Moesia, but this seems in error; the battle was fought outside the jurisdiction of the *magister militum per Thracias*, and it would be more logical for Arnegisclus to have held the supreme command in the region (*magister utriusque militiae*), allowing him to command an army as far as the Utus without leaving his jurisdiction.

The circumstances of the battle suggest a pursuit by Arnegisclus, one for which his cavalry would have come to the fore. The *comitatus* of the *magister militum per Thracias* could notionally call upon more than 27,000 troops – based on the units listed in the *Notitia Dignitatum* and modern-day estimates of unit sizes. The 27,000 troops were based at Marcianopolis, while the *dux* of Moesia Prima could call upon 6,250 men, that of Moesia Secunda 7,000 men of the provincial *limitanei*; Scythia had an additional 8,000 men and Dacia Ripensis a further 8,000 men. If Arnegisclus had every cavalry unit available with him for his pursuit of the Huns in 447, this gives him a cavalry force of some 11,000 men – still a small force and, in reality, it will probably have been smaller still, perhaps only 8,000 men; he cannot have taken every available cavalryman with him. The army of the *magister militum per Thracias* had only seven units of cavalry, however, in comparison to 21 units of infantry, so the number of cavalry could be even fewer still – perhaps just 4,000 men, which was only 15 per cent of the men available.

Employing the arguments outlined above, we may surmise that Arnegisclus could have had other units to bring his numbers up. Regardless, he was vastly outnumbered – and he knew it. His force may have been augmented by the troops of the *comitatus* of Illyricum, another 17,000 troops based at Sirmium (modern-day Sremska Mitrovica, Serbia). This force composition is suggested by Arnegisclus' being given supreme command, rather than simply being *magister militum per Thracias*. Sirmium was, however, 540km from Somovit on the Utus – twice the distance from Somovit to Marcianopolis. Sirmium was also 160km west of Viminacium, where the Huns had crossed the Danube in 441. We have no mention, however, of men of the *magister militum per Illyricum* joining in the battle.

By the late spring and summer of 447 the Huns had already ravaged a great deal of territory with their rapid and terrifying tactics. In addition to the evidence of the *Gallic Chronicle of 452* and Callinicus, Jordanes tells us (*Romana* 331) that Attila had allied himself with the Gepids under Ardaric, the Goths under Walamer (also known as Valamir or Valamer), and other tribes. With these he invaded and ravaged all of the dioceses of Illyria and Thrace, the provinces of Dacia Ripensis and Dacia Mediterranea, Moesia and Scythia. These allies perhaps also suggest different paths of destruction and retreat over the Danube. Marcellinus Comes tells us (*Chronicle* 447)

that the scale of the conflict was greater than that of 443 – an increase in scale suggested by the conquests and alliances Attila had forged after Bleda's death – and that Attila devastated cities and forts across almost the whole of Europa. This was the province around Constantinople and included the Gallipoli peninsula, so perhaps the battles of Callipolis and Sestus should be placed in 447.

Attila's advance was checked at the pass of Thermopylae. From there, Attila turned back towards the Danube where he was met by Arnegisclus at the Utus River in Dacia Ripensis – Marcellinus Comes gives us the details of the location (*Chronicle* 447). Some reconstructions posit that Attila captured cities after the battle of the Utus, but it seems more likely that he took the cities beforehand, and was making his return journey when the Romans met him in battle. If Arnegisclus' objective was pursuit, then cavalry would have been best suited to the task. We saw above that if Arnegisclus had every cavalry unit available to him he would have had a force of 11,000 men, but his cavalry force was probably smaller than this, perhaps only 8,000 men. Hunnic numbers are hard to pin down; modern reconstructions posit a cavalry force as low as 30,000 men, but this seems too low a figure to account for the fear and damage they inflicted on the Romans. This was the first campaign of Attila's newly expanded forces, so perhaps a figure of 50,000 cavalry, as suggested above, is plausible (and it is a figure we can use again as an estimate for the number of Attila's cavalry in 451). If these were the odds Arnegisclus faced, the attack mounted by his 8,000 cavalry can be seen as a desperate bid to target the end of the Hunnic column, heavily laden as it was with plunder.

It is possible that the Hunnic army had broken up into smaller groups at this point to return home with plunder and that Arnegisclus encountered only Attila's portion; but even with the combined *comitatenses* armies of Illyricum and Thrace, Arnegisclus would still have been outnumbered. Another possibility, therefore, is that Arnegisclus made a stand close to the point where the Utus joins the Danube, on the plain north of modern-day Pleven, near modern-day Somovit, where the two rivers join, perhaps expecting that that would be where Attila would cross; in which case we might speculate that Attila aimed to cross over the Danube at modern-day

The Roman fortress of Storgosia (modern-day Pleven, Bulgaria), near the Utus River, may have provided a staging post for Arnegisclus' pursuit of the Huns in 447 and a refuge after it. The battlefield should be sought north of Pleven, at one of the crossings of the modern-day Vit River. (Todor Bozhinov/ Wikimedia/CC BY-SA 3.0)

A 6th-century ring sword, a variation of the *spatha* associated with the Migration Period from the 4th to 7th centuries when Germanic tribes – Goths, Huns, Vandals and Avars – moved into formerly Roman territory. Probably Frankish, this example is from Saint-Dizier, France. (G.Garitan/Wikimedia/CC BY-SA 3.0)

Calinovăț Island, Romania. Alternatively, the location was en route to Viminacium, 415km to the west, or Ratiaria, 190km to the west, both of which were places where the Huns had crossed previously. Making a stand would, however, allow the entire Hun force to come up against Arnegisclus, even if they could not all reach him at once at the river crossing; and there were other crossings which the Huns could take and so bypass Arnegisclus' position. A pursuit to attack the rear of Attila's column would allow Arnegisclus to attack only that part of the column, but the Hunnic units in front might not have been able to re-cross the Utus to fight the Romans. What is more, the Roman armies had been bested by the Huns on several occasions already and so attacking only a portion of them was, perhaps, desirable.

It would seem more likely, therefore, that Arnegisclus pursued Attila's Huns as they withdrew towards the Danube, especially if a portion of the Hunnic host had split off from the main army. Arnegisclus may have learned that the Hunnic army had split onto different paths for the return home and, perhaps, the location of Attila himself. He may have intended to deal a decisive blow to Attila himself.

The sources offer only minimal details about the battle, but it seems to have been fought to a standstill. After the battle the Huns soon withdrew from Roman territory as they had intended; but whether their withdrawal was as a result of the losses inflicted on them or if they simply continued their withdrawal as planned is unclear. Arnegisclus himself fought courageously, but according to Jordanes (*Romana* 331) his horse collapsed under him; he then fought on foot, but was surrounded and eventually cut down. Marcellinus Comes tells us (*Chronicle* 447) that Attila himself killed Arnegisclus, but only after most of the Hunnic army was destroyed. Given the evident security of Attila's rule in the ensuing years and the Hunnic invasions that were to come, not to mention the fact that the Huns were probably already on their return journey to the Danube, wholesale destruction of the Hunnic forces seems unlikely. If only a portion of Attila's forces were with him, however, it is possible that many of these were killed.

On balance, it seems most likely that Arnegisclus pursued Attila's forces as they made their way back to the Danube, the Romans perhaps setting out from the road station at Storgosia, and that they then charged the rear of Attila's column with Arnegisclus' own cavalry at a moment when the majority of Attila's forces were already across the river.

We saw above that the army of the *magister militum per Thracias* included seven units of cavalry, but that these seven units represented only 15 per cent of the men – some 4,000 cavalry – in Arnegisclus' army. If Arnegisclus had called upon every available unit in the diocese, perhaps 20 per cent of the available troops, he might have been able to muster a total of 11,000 cavalry. His actual number of cavalry was probably much smaller, however; I have estimated 8,000 because it makes sense for Arnegisclus to have mustered an all-cavalry army to enable him to pursue the Huns, but he cannot have had every cavalryman available. Even laden with plunder the Huns will have outpaced a partially infantry pursuit. Therefore, to give Arnegisclus the seven cavalry units of his *comitatus* (4,000 men) and an equal number of men from the other cavalry units of the *limitanei* of the diocese of Thrace seems entirely plausible.

Arnegisclus would still have been massively outnumbered, but he might have stood a chance if he struck the rear of the Hun column as it crossed the Utus, thereby not allowing the Huns who had already crossed the river to turn back and come to the aid of the rear of their column. If Attila was isolated, this action may have been intended to kill Attila himself; and if the report of Attila killing Arnegisclus personally can be taken to mean that Attila was in the thick of the battle, this desperate plan may have come close to success. If, however, Arnegisclus had attempted this with only the 4,000 cavalrymen of his *comitatus*, his actions seem futile and even suicidal. Gathering the cavalrymen of the *limitanei* armies will have taken time, as each was based in a separate town – and Arnegisclus did not have time to wait. He probably sent riders out bearing instructions to assemble at Marcianopolis (or perhaps Storgosia); those Roman cavalrymen that arrived in time departed with Arnegisclus' force. We might therefore propose that more units from Dacia Ripensis and Moesia Secunda were present (although Scythia was relatively close to Marcianopolis). The cavalrymen from Moesia Prima and Dacia Ripensis may have been in danger of encountering the Huns travelling west as those cavalry units travelled east towards Marcianopolis, or they may have joined Arnegisclus en route.

A 6th-century *spatha* with scabbard and dagger; this example is from Wünnenberg-Fürstenberg, Germany. Note also the javelin and spearheads (above), the designs of which did vary in shape and size but not greatly, and which were used by many armies, Roman and non-Roman. (T o m/ Wikimedia/FAL)

Arnegisclus at bay

Arnegisclus, the *magister utriusque militiae*, has led an 8,000-strong cavalry force against the Huns as they cross the Utus, weighed down with plunder, on their return to the Hunnic homelands north of the Danube. Arnegisclus has a combination of all the cavalry units available to him – heavy cavalry, horse-archers and medium cavalry. Most of the Hun column has crossed the river already when the Roman cavalry attack, led

by Arnegisclus. The Romans are outnumbered, but use the river to even up the odds; the crossing keeps most of the Huns trapped on the far riverbank, unable to turn back and engage the Romans. Arnegisclus fights in mid-stream, leading his men in a desperate fight against the Hunnic cavalry. His horse is exhausted and wounded, and it collapses under him as the Huns, Attila leading them, close in.

This conjectural cavalry force of 8,000 men therefore gives Arnegisclus the named units of the *comitatus*: the *Comites Arcadiaci*, *Comites Honoriaci* and *Equites Theodosiaci iuniores* (all three *palatini vexillationes*) plus the *comitatus* units of the *Equites catafractarii Albigenses*, *Equites sagittarii seniores*, *Equites sagittarii iuniores* and *Equites primi Theodosiani*. The named cavalry units of the *limitaneus* of Scythia were seven *cunei*: the *Cuneus equitum scutariorum*, *Cuneus equitum Solentium*, *Cuneus equitum stablesianorum* (based at Cii), *Cuneus equitum stablesianorum* (based at Bireo), *Cuneus equitum catafractariorum*, *Cuneus equitum armigerorum* and *Cuneus equitum Arcadum*. The *limitaneus* of Moesia Secunda provided seven more *cunei*: the *Cuneus equitum scutariorum* (based at Securisca), *Cuneus equitum Solentium*, *Cuneus equitum scutariorum* (based at Latius), *Cuneus equitum armigerorum*, *Cuneus equitum secundorum armigerorum*, *Cuneus equitum scutariorum* and *Cuneus equitum stablesianorum*. Eight *cunei* came from Moesia Prima: the *Cuneus equitum Constantiacorum*, *Cuneus equitum promotorum* (based at Flaviana), *Cuneus equitum sagittariorum* (based at Tricornio), *Cuneus equitum Dalmatarum* (based at Aureomonto), *Cuneus equitum promotorum* (based at Viminacio), *Cuneus equitum sagittariorum* (based at Laedenatae), *Cuneus equitum Dalmatarum* (based at Pinco) and *Cuneus equitum Dalmatarum* (based at Cuppis). Dacia Ripensis could provide nine *cunei*: the *Cuneus equitum Dalmatarum Fortensium*, *Cuneus equitum Dalmatarum Divitensium* (based at Dortico), *Cuneus equitum scutariorum* (based at Cebro), *Cuneus equitum Dalmatarum Divitensium* (the location is missing, but probably based at Drobeta), *Cuneus equitum Dalmatarum* (based at Augustae), *Cuneus equitum Dalmatarum* (based at Varina), *Cuneus equitum stablesianorum*, *Cuneus equitum scutariorum* (based at Agete) and *Cuneus equitum Constantinianorum*.

Unfortunately, the shield designs of the Eastern Roman Empire's cavalry units are missing from the *Notitia Dignitatum*, and it does not record the shield pattern of any *limitanei cunei* units, so we cannot know precisely what the shields of these units looked like. It is clear, however, that there were a range of cavalry types present – heavy cavalry, horse-archers and medium cavalry. Most, however, are simply described as *cunei*, irregular units, of cavalry, and we do not know if (or what) their other designations meant, if anything.

The Catalaunian Plains

20 June AD 451

BACKGROUND TO BATTLE

At the conclusion of 447, it seems that Attila was once again paid to leave the Eastern Roman Empire provinces alone in the aftermath of the battle of the Utus. The following year, Marcellinus Comes records (*Chronicle* 448) that Attila sent embassies to Theodosius II demanding payment of the agreed amount. The next we hear of Attila, he was planning to invade the West. In spring 451, Attila turned his attention to invading the Western Roman Empire. The picture presented by the sources is complicated and may contain many false claims and red herrings. In 450 Attila had backed the losing candidate as king of the Visigoths, traditionally an enemy of the Western Roman emperor. Jordanes records (*Getica* 184–86) that Gaiseric, king of the Vandals, somehow persuaded Attila to attack the Visigoths. Many modern-day commentators do not accept this Vandal–Hun alliance, however. By attacking the Visigoths at this moment, Attila claimed to be aiding Rome. According to Gregory of Tours (*Historia Francorum* 2.5), plans for the invasions may have stretched back several years, perhaps soon after 447.

According to Priscus (*History* F20.1, 3) the invasion of the Western Roman Empire was precipitated by Justa Grata Honoria, elder sister of the Western Roman emperor Valentinian III. She wrote to Attila, possibly to avoid a marriage arranged by her brother, asking that Attila 'rescue' her. Attila interpreted this as an offer of marriage and asked Valentinian III for half of the Western Roman Empire as dowry.

Aëtius advised Valentinian III to reject Attila's overtures of friendship, knowing he was putting together a vast alliance (500,000 men) to invade. Jordanes only names the Huns, and 'innumerable people of divers tribes' (*Getica* 198), although he does mention the Ostrogoths under brothers

Valamir, Thuidimer and Vidimer, and the Gepids under their king, Ardaric with 'a countless host' (*Getica* 198–99). Sidonius, however, names several allies of the Huns (*Carmina* 7.321–25), although the trustworthiness of his list has been questioned. Among them he lists the Gepids, Rugi, Sciri, Neuri, Bastarnae, Thuringii, Bructeri, Franks and Burgundians. This suggests that sections of these peoples fought on both sides. Socrates of Constantinople's account of the Burgundians throwing off the Hunnic yoke (*Ecclesiastical History* 7.30) gives a reason for some fighting for and others against the Huns. Aëtius then formed an alliance of his own, summoning troops from the peoples of Gaul and elsewhere – even Britain – and, most importantly, the Visigoths under their new king, Theodoric I.

A gilded glass medallion depicting Galla Placidia with her children. The future Western Roman emperor Valentinian III is on the left. On the right is his older sister, the *augusta* Justa Grata Honoria. Her appeal to Attila and his attitude to the marriage alliance are complex and still highly debated. They may have led to the Hunnic invasion of Gaul in 451 and/or of Italy in 452. (Universal History Archive/Getty Images)

Attila crossed the Rhine River, perhaps near the old Roman fort of Castellum apud Confluentes (modern-day Koblenz, Germany) where the Rhine and the Moselle River join. Many cities claimed in their subsequent histories that Attila sacked them, but few reveal any archaeological traces of destruction at the time. Attila reached Divodurum Mediomatricorum (modern-day Metz, France) on the Moselle, on 7 April; Strasbourg, Worms, Mainz, Trier and Cologne all also claimed to have been his victims. Taking all these cities does not allow a single invasion route, however, and it is possible there were several. After Divodurum Mediomatricorum the Huns took Rheims and then Tongres, although towns to the north – Tournai, Cambrai, Thérouanne, Arras, Amiens and Beauvais – also have historical claims to have been attacked by the Huns. Paris (not a significant city in 451) was probably bypassed although it too has a tradition of a Hunnic siege, in which St Genevieve saved the city.

The Huns' next destination was Aurelianum (modern-day Orléans, France), en route to Toulouse in the south of France and the seat of Visigothic power. Putting the city under siege, and probably using the same techniques he had used at Naissus, Attila was met by the troops of Aëtius' alliance, possibly just as he breached the walls and prepared to storm the city on 14 June. Sidonius, writing in 478 (*Letters* 8.15), states that the city's walls had been breached but that the city was not ruined, perhaps suggesting the timely arrival of the relief army. Gregory of Tours tells us that 'the walls were now trembling from the hammering of the rams and were just about to fall' (*Historia Francorum* 2.7). Forced to withdraw from Aurelianum, Attila was pursued by Aëtius' forces.

Although the army Aëtius summoned was an alliance of Visigoths, Alans and others, he also had Roman troops, especially those based in Gaul. According to Jordanes (*Getica* 189), the Visigoths knew how to defeat Attila and provided 'a countless host' (*Getica* 190 & 199). Theodoric I sent four of his sons home and brought only two with him; Theodoric and Thorismund.

Aëtius' Gallic *comitatus* had 32,000 men and included the 12 cavalry units (each of 500 men: 6,000 Roman cavalry in total) under the command of the *magister equitum per Gallias* based in Gaul. These were in addition to a large number of infantry and other units. As *magister utriusque militiae*, Aëtius had approximately 28,000 men in Mediolanum although not all marched with him. If Aëtius had every cavalry unit available to him he had some 13,000 men. Once again, in reality, he probably had far fewer men, perhaps 10,000. Aëtius' cavalry would have a vital role to play in the battle, however. Sidonius states (*Carmina* 7.329–35) that Aëtius left Italy with no legionaries, only a few meagre *auxilia*, perhaps only a cavalry force. Aëtius expected the Goths to join his camp only to learn that they were awaiting the Huns in their own territory. The Visigoths finally committed to the alliance and marched to join him.

The cavalry of the Visigoths, Franks and Alans were probably provided in large numbers and were very similar in terms of troop types. We do not know what proportions of infantry to cavalry they fielded, but the estimates for the Roman forces can probably be applied. From Arles, the alliance advanced to Aurelianum, arriving just in time. Aëtius may have been subordinate to Theodoric I in the alliance even though most sources credit Aëtius as its instigator and commander. The Visigoths and other allies contributed more forces and Theodoric I was the figurehead, but Aëtius is usually seen as the man in command. This too can perhaps be challenged. Prosper comments (*Epitoma Chronicon* a.434) that the Romans and Goths agreed to combine their forces and that Aëtius, with his great foresight, was able to gather a multitude equal to the Hunnic force. Thus, we see Aëtius credited as the actual leader even if Theodoric I was the highest-ranking commander – and the Visigothic king was given the position of honour on the right of the allied battle line (Jordanes, *Getica* 197), which further reinforces this idea. Cassiodorus, quoting a letter from Theoderic the Great, king of the Ostrogoths (r. 471–526) to Alaric written in *c.*507 (*Variae* 3.1.1), states that, at the Catalaunian Plains, Attila wavered before Visigothic (rather than Roman) strength. This too reinforces the idea that Theodoric I was seen as the leader of the alliance, at least from the perspective of the Franks.

1 On the morning of 20 June 451, Attila draws up his army on the southern side of Les Maures Ridge at Montgueux, 6km west of Tricasses. His left wing consists of the Ostrogoth contingent (**A**) led by their kings Valamir, Thuidimer and Vidimer, and the Gepids (**B**) under their king, Ardaric. Attila himself is in the centre surrounded by his Huns (**C**). Attila's right wing consists of his other allies (**D**) – 'innumerable people of divers tribes' (Jordanes, *Getica* 198) – although Sidonius (*Carmina* 7.321–25) names the Gepids, Rugi, Sciri, Neuri, Bastarnae, Thuringii, Bructeri, Franks and Burgundians. Several of these names are, however, poetic licence and probably of little use.

2 Theodoric I and Aëtius draw up their forces on the northern side of Les Maures Ridge. Theodoric I and his Visigoths are on the right wing (**E**), with Thorismund commanding the cavalry on the Visigoth left (**F**). In the centre are Sangiban and the Alans (**G**) along with 'loyal allies'. These are not named, but probably consisted of the allies named elsewhere (Jordanes, *Getica* 191; Paul the Deacon, *Historia Romana* 14.4): Franks, Sarmatians, Armoricans, Liticians, Burgundians, Saxons, Riparians, Olibriones – 'once Roman soldiers and now the flower of the Roman forces' (Jordanes, *Getica* 191) – Riparioli and Briones. Paul the Deacon adds 'almost the whole people of the West' (*Historia Romana* 14.4). It is not possible to establish whether the order in which these Roman allies are listed is significant and we do not know how they were deployed in this central division. The Roman contingent is on the left wing, with Aëtius and the Roman cavalry (**H**) nearer the centre and the rest of the Roman force (**I**) to their left. The cavalry units available to Aëtius will have consisted of the 12 named units of the *magister equitum per Gallias* and probably others. These 12 were the *Equites Batavi seniores*, the *Equites Cornuti seniores*, the *Equites Batavi iuniores*, the *Equites Brachiati seniores*,

the *Equites Honoriani seniores*, the *Equites Honoriani Taifali iuniores*, the *Equites armigeri*, the *Equites octavo Dalmatae*, the *Equites Dalmatae passerentiaci*, the *Equites prima Gallia*, the *Equites Mauri alites* and the *Equites Constantiani feroces*. Other units include *Comites seniores*, the *Equites promoti seniores*, the *Comites Alani*, the *Equites Mauri feroces* and the *Equites Brachiati iuniores*, possibly brought from Italy.

3 At approximately 1500hrs the battle begins with a race for the ridge crest. Aëtius' and Thorismund's cavalry forces combine and race to the ridge crest, arriving just before a section of the Huns sent by Attila. The remainder of the Roman left, the Visigoth right and the allied centre do not engage. Likewise, the Hun allies on the right and left wings do not engage.

4 The Huns are repulsed at the ridge crest and retreat back towards Attila. This may have been a feigned retreat, but the Romans and Visigoths do not pursue.

5 Attila leads renewed Hun attempts to take the ridge crest. The fighting is fierce and lasts the rest of the day.

6 Theodoric I leads a force to reinforce Thorismund in the centre. He is attacked and cut down by the Ostrogoths.

7 The remaining Visigoths advance and attack the Huns in their left flank, almost reaching Attila himself.

8 Attila calls for a general withdrawal to the Hunnic wagon laager. The Visigoths and Romans pursue into the night. Thorismund is almost trapped in the Hun laager and Aëtius becomes lost, seeking refuge in the Visigoth camp. The Huns remain in their laager.

Battlefield environment

Various locations have been suggested for the battle of the Catalaunian Plains; none has won universal acceptance and several possible sites are given unwavering parochial and partisan support by modern residents. Retiring from Aurelianum for five days, Attila arrived at Tricasses (modern-day Troyes, France) on the Seine River. As he prepared to cross the river by the bridge there, he was met by the forces of Theodoric I and Aëtius. Some sources give the location as close to Metz, or the Mauriac plain, even on the Loire River (or the Danube). Modern scholars have argued incessantly over their favoured location, north, east or west of Troyes. The ancient town of Catalaunum is now Châlons-en-Champagne on the Marne River (hence the battle of Châlons), although the plains thereabouts have no ridges (a feature central to Jordanes' account). Jordanes, our best account of the battle, is vague on the location (*Getica* 192), however, although he gives some very precise measurements

hence the continuing debate as to its location. Jordanes describes the battlefield as a 'plain rising by a sharp slope to a ridge' (*Getica* 197). Later (*Getica* 208), Jordanes also mentions a stream in the plain that ran with blood.

The location of Montgueux, 6km west of Troyes and perhaps known as Les Maures Ridge, was pointed out in 2011 and has sound reasons to support its claim to be the battlefield location. The ridge has caused consternation among scholars, however, with some reconstructions making it the centre of the battlefield while others minimize its role and place the battle on a plain beside it. It seems clear from Jordanes' account, however, that occupation of the ridge and the subsequent struggle to control it was the crux of the battle. He tells us (*Getica* 197) that the Huns seized the right side of the ridge and the Visigoths the left, with the ridge crest untaken; it would be there that the battle was decided.

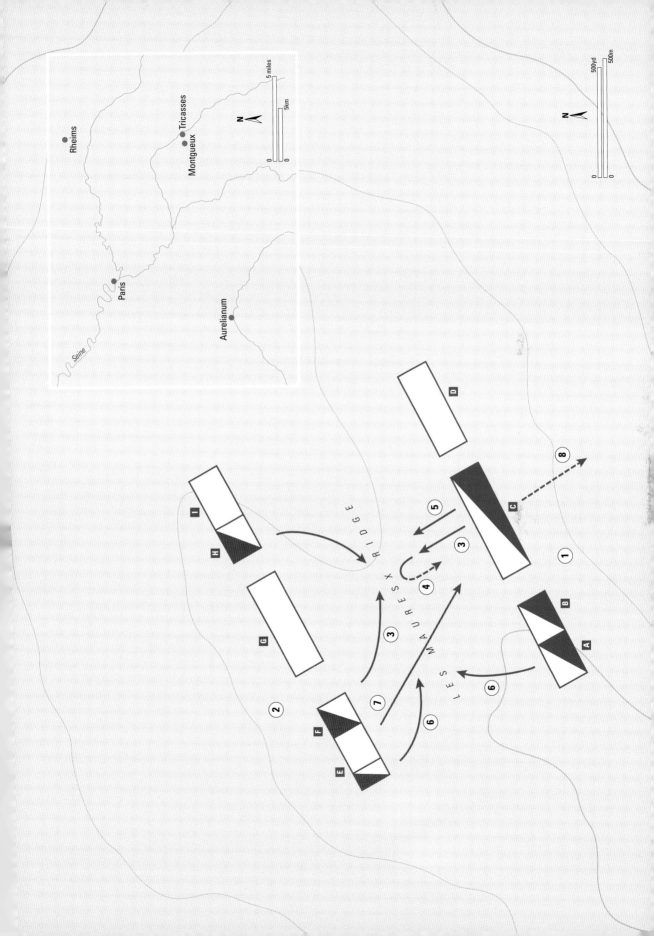

Rheims

Seine

Paris

Montgueux

Tricasses

Aurelianum

N

5 miles
5km

N

500yd
500m

RIDGE

MAURES

LES

A
B
C
D
E
F
G
H
I

1
2
3
4
5
6
7
8

INTO COMBAT

The forces of the Roman–Visigothic alliance caught up with the Huns around 19 June, five days after the withdrawal from Aurelianum. A fight between Attila's Gepids and the Roman-allied Franks resulted in both sides being bloodied, with 15,000 casualties according to Jordanes (*Getica* 217). On the morning of 20 June, the two armies drew up; perhaps the Huns drew up in the dark before dawn as they were known to do (Maurice, *Strategikon* 11.2), although the battle would not start until late in the day and continue into the darkness. Although we have many sources that deal with the battle in vague terms – and these add to the confusion of the actual location and other aspects of the fight – Jordanes' account (*Getica* 182–218) is the most complete we possess.

Jordanes tells us (*Getica* 197) that the Visigoths were stationed on the right wing of the allied army, the Alans (and allies) in the centre and Aëtius on the left. Jordanes introduces the idea that Sangiban, king of the Alans, was suspected of planning to betray Aurelianum to Attila and so was stationed in the allied centre (*Getica* 194–95). Opposite the Romans and their allies, Attila took his place in the centre with the Huns; the men of his alliance, the Ostrogoths and Gepids, made up the wings, the Ostrogoths (or perhaps both) on the left, facing the Visigoths. The reason both contingents may have been on the left wing is that Jordanes says (*Getica* 200) that Attila could trust these kings to fight their kinsmen, the Visigoths. In which case, we do not know which allies occupied the Hunnic right wing.

Jordanes also states (*Getica* 192) that nothing was done under cover, but everything was done in open fight, meaning there was no stratagem or ambush: everything was a straight contest. Nevertheless, Jordanes admits that the conflict was 'complicated and confused' (*Getica* 194). According to Jordanes (*Getica* 195–96), Attila had lost confidence in the face of the additional defences of Aurelianum and withdrew. An augury had then foretold further disaster for the Huns. The same augury, however, stated that 'the chief commander of the foe they were to meet should fall' (Jordanes, *Getica* 196). Attila considered that this must be Aëtius and his death would be welcome, even at the cost of a Hunnic disaster. Attila therefore, according to Jordanes, began the battle – despite his anxiety concerning the impending disaster – at the ninth hour, that is at approximately 1500hrs. This marries with the idea, found in Hydatius (*Chronicle* Olympiad 308/28), that only nightfall closed the battle. The date of 20 June was close enough to the summer solstice to mean that even with a late start, the battle raged for hours – sunset occurred close to 2200hrs and fighting evidently continued into the dark. Allowing for more than seven hours of furious fighting makes the massive casualty numbers reported for the battle more explicable.

Jordanes describes the field as a 'plain rising by a sharp slope to a ridge' (*Getica* 197), which both sides strove to control (*Getica* 201). The fight for the ridge was clearly the most important phase of the battle – it is described as 'the favourable ground' (Jordanes, *Getica* 201), not to be confused with a flat plain as favourable ground for cavalry. Again, Jordanes states explicitly (*Getica* 197) that the Romans held the left side of the ridge, the Huns held the right. The location of the ridge has caused consternation for reconstructers of the battle.

Some modern reconstructions make the ridge the centre of the battlefield, while others minimize its role with the ridge overlooking the battlefield beside it. It is clear from Jordanes' account, however, that the fight for possession of the ridge was the crux of the battle. Jordanes tells us (*Getica* 197) that the Huns seized the steeper right side of the ridge; the Romans under Aëtius, the Visigoths under Theodoric I and their allies seized the less-steep left side and the crest was left unoccupied. Another factor in favour of the ridge being the centre of the battlefield is that it was there that Aëtius, Thorismund and, later, Attila himself fought – this was not a flank of the battle, this was the primary battle site.

According to Jordanes (*Getica* 197), Sangiban was in the Roman–Visigoth centre, surrounded by allies, and thus the suspected confederate of Attila was surrounded by faithful troops. This was an age-old practice going back as far as Homer. Attila and his bravest troops were in the centre of the Hunnic line. Jordanes claims this was for the protection of Attila himself, but, given that the Hunnic king would lead the Huns in their second attempt on the ridge crest, this seems mistaken. Those peoples subject to Attila, 'the innumerable people of divers tribes' (Jordanes, *Getica* 198), were on each wing. Conspicuous among these were the Ostrogoths under Valamir, Thuidimer and Vidimer, and the Gepids under their king, Ardaric, with his 'countless host' (Jordanes, *Getica* 199). Jordanes states that Ardaric and Valamir were Attila's most prized chieftains: '*rex ille famosissimus Ardaricus ... eum et Valamerem, ... super ceteros regulos diligebat*' – 'that most famous king Ardaric ... [Attila] prized him and Valamir ... above all the other chieftains' (*Getica* 199). Some manuscripts replace *famosissimus* with *fortissimus* ('most powerful'), which might imply that Ardaric and Valamir were the commanders of his two remaining wings. This implies, however, that Attila's forces were drawn up in three divisions, like the Romans, which contradicts Maurice's observation (*Strategikon* 11.2) that they only drew up in one. Perhaps the idea of three divisions was the only way a Roman author could make sense of the Hun battle line. The Ostrogoths and Gepids were drawn up against the Visigoths, their kinsmen. Jordanes claims that Valamir was 'a good keeper of secrets', smooth-talking and wily, and Ardaric was 'famed for his loyalty and wisdom' (*Getica* 200). Jordanes is

A view of the terrain around Montgueux. The proximity of Montgueux to Troyes, and the discoveries made there, make it a likely site for the battle in 451. Jordanes gives us a precise measurement of area for the battlefield (100 *leuva* long and 70 *leuva* wide; a plain 150km long by 105km wide). Jordanes' Gallic *leuva* may be a *leuca* or *leuga* from which the league (1½ Roman miles or 2,280m) was derived, giving a larger area of 228km long by 159.6km wide. Paul the Deacon (*Historia Romana* 14.4) concurs with Jordanes' dimensions of the battlefield (100 *leuva* long and 70 *leuva* wide). Again, we can appreciate how a cavalry charge uphill could be far more difficult than it might at first appear. After the repulse of the first Hunnic charge, Attila decided to lead a second with himself at the head. Hard fighting followed and it would seem that Attila only withdrew when his flank was threatened by the Visigoths. (Superjuju10/ Wikimedia/CC BY-SA 3.0)

Attila

Attila was the younger brother of Bleda and the son of Mundzuc, two of whose own brothers (Octar and Ruga) were kings of the Huns. Attila will have been raised as a typical Hun, constantly in the saddle and learning to ride and shoot the bow from a young age. There were clearly extensive diplomatic contacts between the Huns and both halves of the Roman Empire, so the young Attila must have had some awareness of his uncles' political and military expectations.

Jordanes tells us (*Getica* 182) that Attila walked in a haughty and arrogant manner, his eyes moving left and right. Priscus also records (*History* F8.133) that Attila had a flat nose and swarthy complexion with small eyes; his beard was greying and he was short although broad-chested. Attila is described (Jordanes, *Getica* 182) as a lover of war but restrained in action, capable in decision-making; he was gracious to suppliants and offered protection to those who asked. He is, in short, described in the terms of an ideal ruler, although we lack real details of his conduct.

When Octar and Ruga died (in 430 and 434 respectively) Bleda and Attila became kings. They lived in relative peace with Rome for the first few years of their reigns before unleashing their devastating invasions in 441 and 443. Their success and the Romans' willingness to pay tribute probably encouraged yet more invasions.

Attila is accused of murdering (or arranging the murder of) his brother Bleda in about 445, but we do not know enough to be sure. Attila then consolidated his empire and in 447 launched the largest invasion of the Roman Empire yet seen. The Huns were probably paid another tribute to leave, although they had in effect already taken what they wanted.

In 451 Attila invaded the Western Roman Empire, but the reasons for his actions are complicated and difficult to sift. His invasion was immensely successful; he took numerous cities before reaching Aurelianum. Attila's decision to lift the siege of the city has been read as a Hunnic defeat in itself, but it was hardly that. Likewise, the battle of the Catalaunian Plains has been taken as a Hunnic defeat, but it was not – both sides were bloodied, and Attila withdrew only to return in 452, as strong and successful as ever. His withdrawal from Italy in 452 after sacking the cities of the north was remembered as a Christian victory over Attila's paganism, but it probably involved (yet another) massive payment of tribute.

Attila's plans for further conquest were brought to an abrupt halt by his death in 453 amid debated circumstances (haemorrhage, aneurism or murder). Other than splitting his empire between his three sons (Ellac, Dengizich and Ernak), he seems to have left no plans for further conquest.

There are no contemporary depictions of Attila or the Huns. Sometimes credited to the late-15th-century sculptor Giovanni Antonio Amadeo, this is the medallion of Attila in the Certosa di Pavia monastery, Italy, which announces Attila as the 'scourge of God' (*il flagello di Dio*). Note the horns coming out of Attila's head. (Carlo Brogi/Wikimedia/Public Domain)

dismissive of the contingent leaders on Attila's other wing, describing their kings as hanging 'upon Attila's nod like slaves' (*Getica* 200).

Having outlined the dispositions, Jordanes describes the opening of the battle, when Attila dispatched his Huns to take the ridge crest: 'Attila sent his men to take the summit of the mountain, but was outstripped by Thorismund and Aëtius, who in their effort to gain the top of the hill reached higher ground and through this advantage of position easily routed the Huns as they came up' (*Getica* 201). The speed necessary for this action from both sides implies it was undertaken predominantly by cavalry.

Against the cavalry army of the Huns, Thorismund and Aëtius must have urged their combined cavalry forces to seize the ridge crest first. This was a race of horses, and the Roman and Visigothic mounts outpaced the Takhi breed ridden by the Huns. Attila's men were beaten to the ridge crest by the combined cavalry of Aëtius and Thorismund, son of Theodoric I. Their men reached the advantage of the higher ground before the Huns could, probably on account of their gentler approach and the speed of their horses in comparison to the sturdier, but slower, Hunnic mounts.

Reaching the ridge crest first, the Romans and Visigoths were able to repel the Hun assault easily. This repulse threw the Huns into confusion, according to Jordanes (*Getica* 201), but we should remember that the Huns were famed for their feigned-flight tactics (Maurice, *Strategikon* 11.2). The Romans and

Flavius Aëtius

Aëtius, the son of Gaudentius, a man of no rank in Scythia, was born in Durostorum (modern-day Silistra, Bulgaria). His father, a member of the *protectores domestici* (the imperial guard) rose to be *magister equitum*. Aëtius was a hostage of the Visigoth king Alaric between 405 and 408 before becoming a hostage of the Hun king Uldin and then his successor, Charaton. The historian Profuturus Frigiderius states (Gregory of Tours, *Historia Francorum* 2.8) that Aëtius had been enrolled as a *praetorian* – perhaps meaning the *protectores domestici* – as a youth, before his time as a hostage, although he was only aged about nine when he went to the Huns. His time among the warlike Goths and Huns would serve him well in the future.

According to Frigiderius, Aëtius was medium in height and well-proportioned, without any defect. Intelligent and full of energy, an excellent horseman and skilled with both bow and lance, he was able as a soldier and in the arts of peace, and was not swayed by unworthy counsellors. He was patient and ready for any exacting task. Like many earlier descriptions of great generals, we are told that Aëtius scorned danger and was able to endure hunger, thirst and the loss of sleep.

Aëtius rose to be *cura palatii* (governor of the palace) at the court of the usurper Iohannes and was sent to secure Hun allies. Returning to Italy in 425, Aëtius discovered that Iohannes had been killed and that Valentinian III had been installed as emperor of the Western Roman Empire. Aëtius reached an accord with the emperor's mother, Galla Placidia, and was appointed *comes et magister militum per Gallias*. Aëtius married the daughter of Carpilio, who had been *comes domesticorum* (commander of the imperial guard). Promoted to *magister militum*, Aëtius was, by 430, the highest-ranking commander in the Western Roman Empire. He continued to defeat incursions along the Rhine and Danube rivers in the early 430s.

In 432, Aëtius fled to the Huns, especially king Ruga, and with Hun assistance returned to power once again as *comes et magister utriusque militiae*, the supreme military commander in the West. Aëtius married his second wife, Pelagia, the widow of Bonifacius. He continued to fight wars in Gaul alongside a Hunnic contingent acting as *foederati* ('allies'). Many of the Roman allies of 451 were peoples settled within the Roman Empire by Aëtius, defeated factions or those with whom he had agreed an uneasy peace while there was a greater threat in the form of the Huns to deal with. Hailed as the mastermind of victory against Attila in 451, he remained silent in 452 and did not face Attila again. After Attila's death in 453, Valentinian III had him murdered in 454.

Visigoths did not pursue the fleeing Huns and Attila himself was forced to lead a second charge.

We can also, perhaps, reassess Sangiban's role in the second battle line. Rather than being a leader of suspect loyalty to the Roman–Visigothic cause, he may have been stationed there deliberately, in accordance with Maurice's later recommendation (*Strategikon* 2.1) for dealing with feigned retreats. Perhaps the Huns were attempting to draw the Romans and Visigoths off the ridge crest. Jordanes gives Attila an encouraging speech in which the Hunnic king stated that war was natural to the Huns and urging them to attack again boldly: 'See, even before our attack they are smitten with terror. They seek the heights, they seize the hills and, repenting too late, clamour for protection against battle in the open fields' (*Getica* 204). Although it is unlikely that Attila ever made such a speech (which continues for five chapters), such accounts are always impossible to dismiss out of hand. The criticisms Attila reportedly makes of the Romans' manner of making battle and his disdain for their way of waging war may hold some value. Jordanes' Attila comments: 'You know how slight a matter the Roman attack is. While they are still gathering in order and forming in one line with locked shields, they are checked, I will not say by the first wound, but even by the dust of battle' (*Getica* 204–05).

We can imagine the apparently disordered charge of the Hun cavalry uphill towards the Romans at the ridge crest, coming to a unified charge

The so-called Stilicho sarcophagus has been identified – by Hughes (2012) and Atanasov (2014) – as actually belonging to Aëtius. What is more, if it is Aëtius who is depicted, the sarcophagus is almost exactly contemporary with the end of the wars against Attila. Aëtius would therefore be the right-hand figure in the roundel, accompanied by his second wife, Pelagia. Note the scale armour on his sleeve. (Sailko/ Wikimedia/CC BY 3.0)

The fight for the ridge

Roman view: The combined cavalry of Aëtius and Thorismund have just reached the summit of the ridge at the centre of the field of the battle of the Catalaunian Plains, and are preparing to repulse the oncoming advance of the Hunnic forces which are approaching rapidly. The Romans, Visigoths and other allies have drawn up their line in three divisions on the left (north) of the ridge at Montgueux; the Huns have drawn up on the right (south). Realizing that occupying the high ground of the ridge crest will be a crucial contest in the forthcoming battle, Aëtius has advanced with his 12 cavalry units (the shields of the *Equites Honoriani Taifali iuniores* are visible), perhaps numbering 10,000 men in total and combined with the allied cavalry forces of the Visigothic prince, Thorismund. Together, they will stand strong and engage in a missile exchange with the Huns and then engage in hand-to-hand combat for control of the vital high ground.

Hunnic view: The Hunnic cavalry of Attila advance rapidly up the steep slope on the southern (right) side of the Montgueux ridge towards the Roman and Visigoth cavalry. Attila too has realized that controlling the ridge will be of vital importance in the battle. As his men approach on their hardy Takhi horses, the cavalry of the Romans and Visigoths have appeared on the ridge before them, reaching the ridge first on their faster horses. Five Roman units are visible (left to right): the *Equites Batavi iuniores*, the *Equites Batavi seniores*, the *Equites Honoriani* *Taifali iuniores*, the *Equites Dalmatae passerentiaci* and the *Equites Constantiani feroces*. Nevertheless, the Hunnic cavalry press their charge. Urging their horses on, the Huns aim to force the Romans and Visigoths from the ridge crest by throwing missiles and then engaging in ferocious hand-to-hand fighting. What is more, the Huns charge knowing that their king, Attila, looks on from behind. They know that any valorous deeds they perform during the battle will be noticed by their leader and earn them rich rewards.

almost miraculously at the last minute. Missiles will have been thrown and then battle joined in hand-to-hand combat. In attempting to take the ridge crest by assaulting it from the steeper side, the Huns were always at a disadvantage, but their lust for battle and desire to do great martial deeds – especially in company with Attila himself – outweighed any thought of tactical disadvantage. They had won in previous encounters when their reputation alone had put enemies to flight, and they probably thought the same would happen now – but the Romans and their allies held firm.

Jordanes' description does not include much detail: 'Hand to hand they clashed in battle, and the fight grew fierce, confused, monstrous, unrelenting – a fight whose like no ancient time has ever recorded. There such deeds were done that a brave man who missed this marvellous spectacle could not hope to see anything so wonderful all his life long' (*Getica* 207). At this point in the battle, Theodoric I rode forward and met his death in the midst of the fighting; Jordanes gives two versions (*Getica* 209). In the first, Theodoric I was riding out to encourage his men, fell from his horse and was trampled. In the second version, however, the Visigothic king was slain by an Ostrogoth named Andag. In Hydatius (*Chronicle* Olympiad 308/28), Theodoric I died after being thrown to the ground. After the battle, Theodoric I's body was found 'where the dead lay thickest' (Jordanes, *Getica* 214). This implies that he was killed in the fighting against the Ostrogoths rather than being trampled by his own horse. Both John Malalas (*Chronicle* 358/14.10) and the *Chronicon Paschale* (Olympiad 307, 450) tell us that Theodoric I died of an arrow wound. This accords with the idea of the Visigothic king being killed in the fighting, although Hydatius makes all the accounts somewhat reconcilable. What is more, these accounts also tell us that there was close-quarter fighting elsewhere on the battlefield, not just between the Huns and Aëtius and Thorismund's men.

The death of Theodoric I perhaps tells us something of the conduct of the battle. At the outset, Theodoric I was on the Roman–Visigothic right wing, probably with his son Thorismund. Aëtius was on the left wing and Sangiban with the Alans and the other allies was in the centre. In order for Aëtius and Thorismund to join together, we might consider that Aëtius was on the right of the left division and Thorismund on the left flank of the right division – this would allow their joint effort to take the ridge to follow the shortest route. When the cavalry of Aëtius and Thorismund joined and raced for the ridge crest, the forces in the Roman–Visigothic centre remained in place, possibly as well as the Visigoths on the right and the other Romans on the left too. We do not read of their advancing until Theodoric I's advance. It is possible there was fighting on both wings, but Jordanes concentrates on the action in the centre where the battle was decided. The wings may have stayed in position to threaten or prevent the

The so-called diptych of Stilicho in Monza Cathedral may also represent Flavius Aëtius, as argued by Atanasov (2014). The dress and equipment of Roman officers appears to have changed little over much of the Late Roman period. The sword and belt have been identified (Atanasov 2014: 16; Bóna 1991: 238) as Hunnic in keeping with Aëtius' contacts with the Huns prior to 451, perhaps gifts from the Hunnic king Ruga. Aëtius is described variously as the man 'on whom at that time the whole Empire of the West depended' (Jordanes, *Getica* 191) and 'Aëtius the Liberator of the Loire' (Sidonius, *Letters* 7.12). Sidonius calls Attila, by contrast, 'Attila the enemy on the Rhine' (*Letters* 8.15). (Leemage/Getty Images)

Hun wings – Ostrogoths and Gepids on the left, other allies on the right – from advancing.

Jordanes tells us (*Getica* 207) that the fighting in the centre was fierce. It is probable that at some point later in the battle, Theodoric I moved to reinforce Thorismund in the centre and that this move was countered by the Ostrogoths. If both Aëtius and Thorismund raced to the ridge crest in the centre with their cavalry forces, they will have left the majority of the forces in place on the wings – the Visigoths under Theodoric I and the Romans under a subordinate commander (who is not named in the Roman tradition). The advance of Theodoric I 'riding to encourage his army' (Jordanes, *Getica* 209) should therefore probably be read as a move to reinforce the centre as Attila led a renewed Hunnic attack. This move may have been observed by the Ostrogoths and they attacked the Visigothic king as he moved forward to reinforce Thorismund. Jordanes then tells us that after Theodoric I had fallen, the Visigoths, 'separating from the Alans' (*Getica* 210), fell upon the horde of Huns and nearly slew Attila. This phrase does seem to imply that the Visigoths and Alans were still in place and that the fight on the ridge crest was largely between the Huns and the (cavalry) troops of Aëtius and Thorismund. The Ostrogoths may have withdrawn after the success of their charge against Theodoric I, leaving the Hunnic flank exposed, or Theodoric I's death may have prompted the remaining Visigoths to charge, dispersing the Ostrogoths and striking the exposed flank of the Huns.

According to Jordanes (*Getica* 217), the Gepids and Franks had fought an encounter the day before the battle, in which 15,000 casualties were suffered. Perhaps the reason that both of these contingents are absent from the accounts of the battle of the Catalaunian Plains is that, nursing their wounds, they took little part in the fighting other than standing in the battle line. This reinforces the idea that the wings did not move and that the struggle for the ridge in the centre decided the battle. Most modern reconstructions have posited a role for the Gepids and Franks, but in Jordanes' account, the battle was in the main between the Huns and the combined forces of Thorismund and Aëtius, with some involvement of the remaining Visigoths and Ostrogoths. The Alans may have stayed out of the fighting altogether, along with the Gepids, in which case the picture of the battle in Jordanes is (perhaps) a comprehensive one – although we are told of other casualties (such as the bodies piled around Theodoric I), perhaps suggesting that there was also close-quarter fighting elsewhere on the battlefield; but those corpses could well have been in the centre where Theodoric I was attempting to reinforce Thorismund.

Jordanes tells us (*Getica* 210) that when the Visigoths nearly reached Attila, he prudently took flight and withdrew to his wagon laager. Jordanes is at pains to criticize this move by Attila, but this was the Huns' usual camp; what is more, returning to such a laager after a close fight had long been their habit. It is clear that both Visigothic and Roman forces conducted a pursuit of the Huns from the ridge crest. Thorismund pursued them, possibly in search of vengeance for the death of his father, although the Visigothic king's body was not discovered until later and it is likely that Thorismund did not yet know of his father's death. According to Jordanes, Thorismund 'came unwittingly to the wagons of the enemy in the darkness of night' (*Getica*

211). For Thorismund to pursue the enemy into the dark and get lost seems peculiar, but it may imply both the confusion of the action in the Hunnic rout/withdrawal and that the battle continued after night fell. It might also suggest that Attila's decision to withdraw was due to the time of day, rather than as a result of any enemy action. At the Hunnic laager, Thorismund was wounded and dragged from his horse but rescued by some of the men with him. There was confusion elsewhere on the battlefield too. Aëtius also became separated from his men and 'wandered about in the midst of the enemy' (Jordanes, *Getica* 212), ending up in the camp of the Visigoths, where he spent the night. The battle would later be represented as a great Roman–Visigothic victory, but the confused end to the fighting suggests that the outcome was much less clear cut.

Jordanes tells us (*Getica* 217) that 165,000 men were slain on both sides in the battle, while Hydatius (*Chronicle* Olympiad 308/28) records 300,000 dead. Jordanes also claims (*Getica* 218) that 15,000 died when the Gepids and Franks clashed on the day before the battle. Paul the Deacon (*Historia Romana* 14.6) adds Jordanes' numbers together to give 180,000 casualties (most of Paul's account follows Jordanes'). These numbers are probably too high, but the battle was undoubtedly very bloody. Jordanes prefaces these losses by calling the battlefield *area innumerabilium populorum*, 'the graveyard of nations' (*Getica* 192). We have reduced Jordanes' numbers by a factor of 10, so his 500,000 becomes 50,000 men. The casualties too can be reduced by a similar factor, suggesting somewhere between 16,500 and 30,000. These are still huge numbers, perhaps suitably so to match the reports of the massive loss of life.

We can briefly explore other accounts of the battle. For the most part they add more confusion than clarity but do provide fragments of useful information. Gregory of Tour's account of the battle is brief but useful. He states (*Historia Francorum* 2.7) that it was Aëtius and Thorismund who won the victory and destroyed the enemy. This corroborates Jordanes' picture of

A 5th- or 6th-century Visigothic belt buckle from Toulouse, France, now in the Henri Prades Archaeological Museum (Musée archéologique Henri-Prades), Montpellier, France. Similar to Late Roman military belt buckles, it reinforces the point that much of the equipment of the allies at the Catalaunian Plains will have been very similar even if artistic details vary slightly. (Christelle Molinié/Wikimedia/CC BY-SA 4.0)

the crux of the battle being the fight for the ridge crest. Hydatius records (*Chronicle* Olympiad 308/28) that the Huns were cut down in open battle and defeated with the aid of God, by the *dux* Aëtius and King Theodoric I (in that order). Battle continued until stopped by nightfall; 300,000 men fell, including Theodoric I. Prosper writes (*Epitoma Chronicon* a.434, 451) of the incalculable slaughter of the battle; it appeared that the Huns were defeated because the survivors lost their taste for fighting and turned for home. Like Jordanes, Paul the Deacon has Attila enlisting the services of a soothsayer regarding the outcome of the forthcoming battle but, hearing that the leader of the enemy would fall (and assuming it to be Aëtius), he 'did not hesitate to commit' (*Historia Romana* 14.5). This differs from Jordanes' account (*Getica* 196), which portrays Attila as being disturbed and anxious.

After the battle, the body of Theodoric I was found 'where the dead lay thickest' (Jordanes, *Getica* 214). The Visigoths mourned their king. Jordanes presents what happened next as the cunning action of Aëtius. The Roman advised Thorismund to secure his own throne and so withdraw from the field (*Getica* 215–16); Thorismund had wanted to annihilate the Huns in vengeance for his father's death. According to Jordanes (*Getica* 216), Aëtius' fear was that if the Huns were destroyed then the Visigoths would turn against the Romans, so recently their enemies. He therefore advised Thorismund to protect his own claim to the Visigothic throne by returning to his capital, Tolosa (modern-day Toulouse, France), to claim his kingship. The reality is probably that Theodoric I's death caused a succession crisis for the Visigoths and Thorismund needed to withdraw to Tolosa anyway. The Visigoth and Roman forces had probably both been severely bloodied, as had the Huns, and it is possible that neither side could fight on. Otherwise, Aëtius allowing the Visigoths (and Franks) to withdraw makes little sense. The Huns did not attack the remaining Roman forces, but neither did the Romans attack the Hunnic wagon laager. The withdrawal of the Visigoths may have allowed Aëtius to claim the victory as his, especially in his dealings with Valentinian III. Paul the Deacon also states (*Historia Romana* 14.5–8) that the battle ended because of nightfall and records that Thorismund determined on besieging Attila in his wagon laager in revenge for the death of his father, but Aëtius dissuaded him and urged him to secure his crown. Gregory of Tours also has Aëtius encourage Thorismund to secure the throne against his brother 'by a stratagem' (*Historia Francorum* 2.7); according to Gregory, Aëtius also caused the king of the Franks to leave – perhaps evidence of the further disintegration of the alliance, one only Sidonius called fragile (*Carmina* 7, 321–35). Gregory has Aëtius collect much booty and return to Italy; Attila, he states, retreated with few men (*Historia Francorum* 2.7).

Attila had remained in his wagon laager and the Huns did not venture out on the day after the battle, although Jordanes states that he threatened to attack: 'this warlike king at bay terrified his conquerors' (*Getica* 212). Attila was far from beaten, however. The Romans and Visigoths decided to besiege his wagon laager (Jordanes, *Getica* 213) but this does not seem to have taken place, perhaps through the disintegration of the alliance or because there were not enough troops left to do so.

Analysis

HUNNIC EFFECTIVENESS

Writing in about 451, Nestorius, the former bishop of Constantinople, offers a perceptive contemporary judgement of Attila's crucial role as the sole Hunnic ruler (*Bazaar of Heracleides* 366–68). Prior to Attila's reign, the Huns (Nestorius calls them 'Scythians') were a nuisance, to be treated as robbers, but when they were united as a kingdom they grew strong and became a great threat, surpassing the combined forces of the Romans.

There has been a trend in recent years to denigrate the accomplishments of Attila, no longer seeing him as a capable general. This study is not the place to argue against that, but it is undeniable that for the greater part of a decade Attila was unstoppable. Many of the Hunnic strengths upon which he would draw in the 440s and 450s were already evident by the time he became king but, looking at his campaigns in 441, 443, 447, 451 and 452, he was able to ravage and plunder unchecked across vast swathes of Roman territory.

The main tool in Attila's achievements was the Hunnic cavalryman and the ever-reliable Takhi upon which he rode to war. Man for man, the Hunnic warrior was clearly a formidable fighter – in combat the Hunnic cavalry repeatedly defeated their Roman opponents. At the Catalaunian Plains, although the Romans and their allies were able to fight the Hun cavalry to a standstill, it is clear that this was not the result of any defect in the Hunnic cavalry: they spent the greater part of the battle trying to take the ridge crest, fighting uphill and at a disadvantage the entire time, and probably coming close to success on more than one occasion, if we read the reinforcement of Theodoric I and then the Visigoths in such a way. The Hunnic cavalry would return to be unstoppable in 452.

A gold Hunnish horse-head fibula, now in the Walters Art Museum. While the design reveals the importance of the horse to Hunnic culture, and the short mane suggests the breed of Hunnic horse, the fibula itself – for pinning cloaks – was a Roman influence on Hunnic culture. As Vegetius and Maurice suggest, both cultures influenced the other. (Walters Art Museum/Wikimedia/ Public Domain)

The Huns could also turn their hand to siege warfare, the storming of Naissus being a notable example of Hunnic success in such fighting. These were the same men who, on horseback, put Roman armies of East and West to flight on multiple occasions.

The Huns' mobility and speed gave them a crucial advantage, allied with their evident understanding of the geography of the Roman world. The routes of Hun advance, along the *via militaris* and across Thrace and other parts of the Roman Empire, show that these raids were carefully thought out, not just random acts of violence. The timing of the Hunnic invasion of 441 suggests a nuanced appreciation of the optimal time to attack, while the Hunnic decision in 443 to target Ratiaria and Naissus – both of them containing Roman armaments factories – at the outset of the campaign demonstrates the sophistication of Hunnic thinking. There was clearly high-level contact between the Huns and both halves of the Roman Empire, and such knowledge of what was going on within the Roman world should not surprise us.

The Huns were able to advance vast distances and capture huge stores of wealth, including slaves and livestock. They did not seem to be interested in incorporating Roman territory into the Hunnic domains, instead being content to return repeatedly in the search for plunder. The stories in our sources of Attila's supposed ambition to become co-emperor of the Western Roman Empire do not sit well with the realities of Hunnic activity, but rather reflect the Roman elite's fears and the commentators' uncertainty about Attila's motives. Likewise, any role Christianity performed in the defeat (or deflection) of Hun activity and Attila in particular has been overplayed in the historical tradition. It was Isidore of Seville, writing in the 7th century (*Origines* 29), who first called the Huns a scourge, which led on to the idea (still prevalent) of Attila as the 'scourge of God' (*flagellum Dei*).

ROMAN EFFECTIVENESS

The Roman armies of the wars against the Huns were still capable of victory. In the years since the Gothic invasions of the 370s the Roman cavalry had learned many lessons in horsemanship from their enemies and incorporated them into their practices. Parties of Huns had fought as Roman allies for decades and the Romans should have been familiar with their tactics. When it came to facing the Huns, however, the Romans seem to have been incapable of mounting an effective battlefield response.

Whereas the Goths had seldom attempted to capture Roman cities and were almost universally unsuccessful when they did try to do so, the Huns showed as early as 441 that they were capable of taking cities of almost any size. Only Constantinople – and perhaps Aurelianum if we accept that the city's walls were not breached – successfully withstood a Hunnic siege. In this the Romans severely underestimated their opponents; the prejudices and biases evident in the sources reveal that the Romans, in both East and West, continued to be incapable of appreciating the capabilities or potential of their Hunnic enemies.

The Hun incursions and the sheer pace of their advance continued to catch the Romans on the back foot. Roman city walls were no defence, but the emperor's commanders persisted with the same methods for a decade – and for most of the decade the result was the same: defeat. At Aurelianum there is some evidence that extra measures were taken in the city's defence, but the precise dating of the strengthening of other walls doesn't allow us to date such measures specifically to the era of the Hunnic invasions. On at least three occasions (and probably more) the only way the Romans could secure peace with the Huns was by agreeing to pay them a tribute in gold. This tribute increased in size each time it was demanded, but it remained unpaid; this led to further invasions. The sources decry the alleged treachery of the Huns in breaking treaties, but it seems clear that the Romans did not honour their end of such agreements.

Another challenge afflicting the Roman armies was a shortage of manpower. This was not a question of the number of troops under arms at any given time; there were large numbers of Roman soldiers available. The intractable problem was concentrating all of the available manpower in one place where it could be used to counter the Huns as they advanced into Roman territory. The armies of individual provinces or dioceses could do nothing to halt the Hunnic advance: the events of the 440s and early 450s showed that the *comitatenses* and *limitanei* armies could not stand up to the numbers of Huns sent against them. Roman infantry seem to have been ineffective and even combined armies of cavalry (such as that possibly deployed at the Utus) were not enough. The Huns were stopped at Thermopylae in 447, but this was because they were not made aware of the mountain path around the pass.

Held in the Museum of Byzantine Art (Museum für Byzantinische Kunst), Bode Museum, Berlin (inv. 4782), this 5th-century wooden sculpture of the relief of a city reveals details of fortifications, shield designs, helmets, and armour types. (Anagoria/Wikimedia/ CC BY 3.0)

It is very difficult to gain an understanding of Roman battlefield effectiveness. For most of the fighting we are poorly informed and the battles only exist as names or numbers. Only at the Catalaunian Plains, where an unprecedented Roman–Visigothic alliance could be mustered, were the Romans and their allies able to fight the Huns to a standstill – and that was a close-run thing. There is evidence that the alliance took years to organize but fell apart very quickly.

There seem to have been capable generals in command of Roman forces, although in their encounters with the Huns they are not portrayed in their best light. Only Aëtius comes out favourably, but there are clouds over his reputation – he could and did use Hunnic forces to his own advantage in order to secure his position, and he may have exploited his supposed 'victory' at the Catalaunian Plains to this end. In 452, the alleged victor of 451 would prove to be stunningly ineffectual, leaving the Romans no option but to resort to the payment of tribute. Fortunately for the Romans, Attila died in 452/53 and his empire, left to his sons, destroyed itself. It would take a new generation of Roman soldiers to rediscover their battlefield effectiveness.

Aftermath

Although many subsequent accounts claimed (and have continued to claim) that Attila was defeated at the Catalaunian Plains (e.g. Gibbon 1781: 1089; Creasy 1851: 144), this seems far from the case and at best the battle appears to have been a bloody draw, with both sides needing to withdraw in order to recoup their losses.

In 452, Prosper records (*Epitoma Chronicon* a.435) that Attila restored his losses of 451 and invaded Italy by way of Pannonia; Italy was in no position to resist. Aëtius was unable to prevent or defeat Attila's invasion, perhaps keeping his army at Bononia (modern-day Bologna, Italy) to block a passage through the Apennines towards Rome. It is possible that Attila's advance was slowed by a Roman shadowing force, troops sent by the new Eastern Roman emperor, Marcian (r. 450–57); the fact that Marcian had to send troops to the Western Roman Empire at all speaks of the magnitude of losses on the Roman side at the Catalaunian Plains. Aëtius did not possess a victorious army, brimming with confidence after that 'victory', but one that would not face Attila in open battle again and needed propping up by Eastern Roman Empire troops. What is more, the sources suggest that the Huns overran the north of Italy without much resistance. Prosper states (*Epitoma Chronicon* a.435) that Aëtius made no provisions following the exertions of 451 and failed to make use of the barriers of the Alps by which the enemy could have been checked. Instead, he proposed a full retreat from Italy, a suggestion Prosper calls disgraceful and shameful (*Epitoma Chronicon* a.435).

Jordanes' is the best account of the events of 452 despite having Attila move on Italy immediately after the Catalaunian Plains. Jordanes claims that Attila's first move was to attack Aquileia with a 'long and fierce' siege (*Getica* 219). He tells us that the Huns 'constructed battering rams and bringing to bear all manner of engines of war, they quickly forced their way into the city, laid it waste, divided the spoil, and so cruelly devastated it as scarcely to leave a trace to be seen' (*Getica* 221). The Huns raged through the remaining cities

of the Veneti (though Jordanes does not name them); Mediolanum was 'laid waste' (*Getica* 221), as was Ticinum.

Paul the Deacon records a similar story (*Historia Romana* 14.9) of Aquileia being taken with the use of machines and engines: resources were plundered, citizens captured or slaughtered and the city put to the flame. Paul then claims that 'all the cities of Venetia' (*Historia Romana* 14.11) were subjected to similar treatment – named as Patavium, Vicentia, Verona, Brixia, Bergamum, Mediolanum and Ticinum.

Jordanes tells us (*Getica* 222) that Attila intended to reach Rome, although it is hard to see why this would be so in the mid-5th century when Rome no longer held any political role. Paul tells us (*Historia Romana* 14.11) that Attila camped where the Mincius River (now the Mincio River in Italy) flowed into the Padum River (now the Po River in Italy). This will have been near Mantua, past which the Mincius flowed. There, according to Paul, the Romans sent an embassy. While Paul credits Pope Leo I (*Historia Romana* 14.12–13) with the success of the mission to Attila, Prosper (*Epitoma Chronicon* a.435) also includes two prominent politicians, the *praefectus* Trigetius and the consul of 450 Gennadius Avienus, and records that Attila ordered the war to be halted, promised peace and retired beyond the Danube.

Attila did not gain what he had been hoping for – he received neither the hand of Honoria in marriage nor part of the Western Roman Empire as dowry. In all probability he was paid off with vast sums of gold, just as he had been in the past. His retiring in 452 may therefore suggest that his claims of marriage and dowry were simply pretexts. That said, only Procopius suggests (*Vandal Wars* 3.4.29) that Attila gained tribute payment at this time; but his account is so muddled as to be almost useless – for instance, he inexplicably places Attila's taking of Aquileia after the death of Aëtius (*Vandal Wars*

Remains of a Roman tower in the walls of Mediolanum. According to Jordanes (*Getica* 222), these fortifications could not withstand the Hunnic siege of 452. Mediolanum was a much more important city than Aquileia and yet the latter's fall to Attila is given more emphasis in the sources. This could suggest that Aquileia's role as the headquarters of the *Claustra Alpium Iuliarum* meant that it was seen as a greater loss. (Ugodiamante/Wikimedia/CC BY-SA 4.0)

3.4.30). Attila's forces may also have suffered from plague and disease; a famine in the north of Italy in 451 would have meant there was little food or fodder for his army. All of these factors probably led to his withdrawal, but chief among them was probably the one which largely escapes mention in the sources: a very generous payment in gold.

There is little doubt that the news of Attila's death in 453 was a turning point for both sides. Marcellinus Comes does not refer to the battle of the Catalaunian Plains at all and for 452 only mentions the destruction of Aquileia (*Chronicle* 452), but for the year 453/54, the news that Attila had died is of the foremost importance. Marcellinus Comes' version of events (*Chronicle* 453) is that Attila was stabbed in the night by his wife, but he reports that others said the Hunnic king died from coughing up blood. The second noteworthy event of that year was that Aëtius was killed, cut down in the palace on the orders of Valentinian III; Hydatius claims (*Chronicle* Olympiad 308/30) Aëtius' assassination was at the emperor's own hand. These two events are therefore linked and Marcellinus Comes' rejoinder makes clear the importance he attached to Aëtius' death. He states that with his death the Western Roman Empire also fell; it had yet to be restored at the time when Marcellinus Comes was writing in the 530s – indeed he was prescient that it would never be restored. Marcellinus Comes therefore viewed Aëtius (rightly or wrongly) as the defender of the West. With Aëtius' assassination – after the threat of Attila had conveniently disappeared – we see the continued short-sightedness of Western rulers who viewed strong military commanders upon whom until very recently they had relied, as threats to their throne.

There is not the space to examine Attila's death in depth here, but there can be no doubt that this event saved the Romans from further Hunnic depredations. Attila's empire was divided among his three sons, Ellac, Dengizich and Ernak, but they fought among themselves and never posed the threat their father had. Ellac, killed at the battle of Nedao in 454 when the Huns fought their former Ostrogothic vassals, was succeeded by Ernak. He and Dengizich sent embassies to Constantinople in 465–66, but Dengizich refused to negotiate with Anagast, the son of Arnegisclus, who was *magister militum per Thracias* in the 460s. In 467 Dengizich was determined to take Constantinople and crossed the Danube, but he was defeated and killed in battle in either 468 or 469. The days when the Huns posed an existential threat to Rome were over.

BIBLIOGRAPHY

Sources

Most of our sources on the Huns are fragmentary or only deal with them briefly. Chief among the authors is **Priscus of Panium**, who visited Attila's court in 448; his surviving account of that visit (probably written in about 476) is the most famous fragment of his work.

The 6th-century historian **Jordanes** wrote two useful works. Known as the *Getica*, *De origine actibusque getarum* ('On the Origin and Deeds of the Goths') also includes Hunnic history. Jordanes also wrote a *Romana*, a short history of the most noteworthy events in Rome's history down to 552. Also useful is the *Historia Gothorum* by **Isidore of Seville**, written in the 7th century.

The 4th-century AD writer **Ammianus Marcellinus** refers to the Huns as the reason for the Goths crossing into the Roman Empire in 376 in his work the *Rerum gestarum libri* (known as the *Res gestae*). Other 4th-century historians such as **Eunapius** give us similar insights, although the Greek historian **Zosimus** made use of Eunapius in his *Nea Historia* (*New History*) and later added material on the Huns to it. **Olympiodorus of Thebes** wrote a history called *Gle Syggrathes* ('Raw material for History') covering the years 407–25; surviving fragments include useful information on the Huns. The translator of the Bible into Latin, **Jerome**, also includes some useful observations in his letters and commentaries, as does the bishop of Mediolanum, **Ambrose**.

Several contemporaries referred to the events of Hunnic invasions in their writings, notably **Sidonius Apollinaris**, author of *Carmina* 7, a panegyric on the emperor Avitus (r. 455–56). Another contemporary was **Hydatius**, who wrote a *Chronicle* of the 4th and 5th centuries. **Prosper Tiro**, also known as Prosper of Aquitaine, wrote his *Epitoma Chronicon* between 433 and 455.

Gregory of Tours wrote the *Historia Francorum* ('History of the Franks,' actually titled *Decem Libri Historiarum* 'Ten Books of Histories') in the late 6th century. His history necessarily includes the Huns and Attila in Book 2.

The *Chronicon Paschale* (*Easter Chronicle*) is a 7th-century work that briefly includes the Huns. **Marcellinus Comes** wrote a *Chronicle* that focuses on the Eastern Roman Empire from 379 to 534. Other useful chronicles include the anonymous *Gallic Chronicle of 452* and the *Chronicle of 511*. Also helpful is the *Chronicle* of **John Malalas**, written in the mid-6th century. Church histories such as the *Ecclesiastical Histories* of **Sozomen**, **Socrates of Constantinople** and **Theodoret** also contain information not preserved elsewhere; so too **Nestorius**' *Bazaar of Heracleides*. Some of the edicts of Theodosius II preserved in the *Theodosian Code* can also be used.

A work by **Cassiodorus** called *Variae* makes reference (*Variae* 1.4.11–12) to an embassy to Attila undertaken by his great-grandfather (also named Cassiodorus), together with Carpilio, Aëtius' son, *c*.435–40. Evidence from this visit no doubt informed Cassiodorus' lost *Gothic History* (*Variae* 9.25.5), which was one of Jordanes' main sources.

Two military treatises, the *De Re Militari* of **Vegetius** and the *Strategikon* of the Byzantine emperor **Maurice** (r. 584–602), offer valuable insights. The *Notitia Dignitatum* (*List of Offices*) provides details of the organization of the Eastern (*Orientis*) and Western (*Occidentis*) empires.

Several other sources are useful for their brief observations. The *Historia Romana* of **Paul the Deacon** (Paulus Diaconis) in the 8th century is useful, although as yet untranslated. Paul used Jordanes as a source, but there are sections in which his work deviates from or gives more information than Jordanes, possibly reflecting another source (perhaps Cassiodorus). The situation is the same with **Callinicus**' *Vita Hypatii* (*Life of Saint Hypatius*). **Procopius**, a Byzantine historian writing in the mid-6th century, wrote about the wars of the preceding age. While much of his information about Attila is very muddled, he can be used with caution. The fragments of **John of Antioch** (as well as preserving Priscus), writing in the 7th century, can also be useful.

Ancient works

Agathias, 'The Histories', trans. J.D. Frendo (1975), in *Corpus Fontium Historiae Byzantinae* – Series Berolinensis, vol. 2A. Berlin: Walter de Gruyter.

Ambrose, *Letters*, trans. H. Walford (1881), in *Library of the Fathers of the Holy Catholic Church*. Oxford: James Parker & Co.

Ammianus Marcellinus, *Rerum gestarum libri*, trans. C.D. Yonge (1862). London: Henry. G. Bohn.

Cassiodorus, *Variae, Letters*, trans. S.J.B. Barnish (1992). Liverpool: Liverpool University Press.

Chronicon Paschale, trans. M. & M. Whitby (1989). Liverpool: Liverpool University Press.

Claudian, *Poems*, trans. M. Platnauer (1922). Two volumes. Cambridge, MA & London: Harvard University Press.

Eunapius, *Historia* (Fragments), trans. R.C. Blockley (1983), in *The Fragmentary Classicising Historians of the Later Roman Empire*. Cambridge: Francis Cairns.

Gallic Chronicle of 452, trans. A.C. Murray (2000), in *From Roman to Merovingian Gaul: A Reader*. Peterborough: Broadview Press.

Gregory of Tours, *History of the Franks*, trans. E. Brehaut (1916). New York, NY: Columbia University Press.

Herodotus, *The Histories*, trans A.D. Godley (1920–25). Four volumes. Cambridge, MA & London: Harvard University Press.

Hydatius, *Chronicle*, trans. R.W. Burgess (1993). Oxford: Clarendon Press.

Isidore of Seville, *History of the Kings of the Goths, Vandals, and Suevi*, trans. G. Donini & G.B. Ford (1966). Leiden: E.J. Brill.

Jerome, *Letters*, trans. W.H. Fremantle, G. Lewis and W.G. Martley (1893), in *Nicene and Post-Nicene Fathers*, Second Series, Vol. 6. Buffalo, NY: Christian Literature Publishing Co.

John Malalas, *Chronicle*, trans. E. Jeffreys, M. Jeffreys & R. Scott (1986). Melbourne: Australian Association for Byzantine Studies.

John of Antioch, *Historia chronike*, trans. Sergei Mariev, in *Ioannis Antiocheni fragmenta quae supersunt omnia* (2008), *Corpus Fontium Historiae Byzantinae* – Series Berolinensis, vol. 47. Berlin: Walter de Gruyter.

Jordanes, *The Gothic History*, trans. C.C. Mierow (1915). Princeton, NJ: Princeton University Press.

Jordanes, *Romana*, trans. P. Van Nuffelen & L. Van Hoof (2020). Liverpool: Liverpool University Press.

Marcellinus Comes, *Chronicle*, trans. B. Croke (1995). Sydney: Australian Association for Byzantine Studies.

Maurice, *Strategikon*, trans. G.T. Dennis (1984). Philadelphia, PA: University of Pennsylvania Press.

Nestorius, *The Bazaar of Heracleides*, trans. G.R. Driver (1925). Oxford: Clarendon Press.

Olympiodorus, *Historia* (Fragments), trans. R.C. Blockley (1983), in *The Fragmentary Classicising Historians of the Later Roman Empire*. Cambridge: Francis Cairns.

Pacatus, *Speeches*, trans C.E.V. Nixon & B. Rodgers (1994), in *In Praise of Later Roman Emperors*. Berkeley, CA: University of California Press.

Priscus of Panium, *Histories*, trans. J. Given (2014). Merchantville, NJ: Evolution Publishing. Another translation by R.C. Blockley (1983), in *The Fragmentary Classicising Historians of the Later Roman Empire*. Cambridge: Francis Cairns.

Procopius, *History of the Wars*, trans. H.B. Dewing (1914–28). Five volumes. Cambridge, MA & London: Harvard University Press.

Procopius, *On Buildings*, trans. H.B. Dewing (1940). Cambridge, MA & London: Harvard University Press.

Prosper Tiro, *Epitoma Chronicon*, trans. A.C. Murray (2000), in *From Roman to Merovingian Gaul: A Reader*. Peterborough: Broadview Press.

Rufinus, *Ecclesiastical History*, trans. W.H. Fremantle (1892), in P. Schaff & H. Wace, eds, *Nicene and Post-Nicene Fathers*, Second Series, Vol. 3. Buffalo, NY: Christian Literature Publishing Co.

Sidonius, *Letters*, trans. O.M. Dalton (1915). Two volumes. Oxford: Clarendon Press.

Sidonius Apollinaris, *Poems, Letters*, trans. W.B. Anderson (1939–65). Two volumes. Cambridge, MA & London: Harvard University Press.

Socrates, *Ecclesiastical History*, trans. A.C. Zenos (1890), in P. Schaff & H. Wace, eds, *Nicene and Post-Nicene Fathers*, Second Series, Vol. 2. Buffalo, NY: Christian Literature Publishing Co.

Sozomen, *Ecclesiastical History*, trans. E. Walford (1855). London: Henry G. Bohn.

Tacitus, *Annales*, trans. J. Jackson (1931). Four volumes (with *Historiae*, trans. C.H. Moore, 1925–37). Cambridge, MA & London: Harvard University Press.

Tacitus, *Germania*, trans. M. Hutton (1914). Cambridge, MA & London: Harvard University Press.

Theodoret, *Ecclesiastical History*, trans. B. Jackson (1892), in P. Schaff & H. Wace, eds, *Nicene and Post-Nicene Fathers*, Second Series, Vol. 3. Buffalo, NY: Christian Literature Publishing Co.

Theodosian Code, trans. C. Pharr (1952), in *The Theodosian Code and Novels and the Sirmondian Constitutions: A Translation with Commentary,*

Glossary, and Bibliography. Princeton, NJ: Princeton University Press.

Vegetius, *Epitome of Military Science*, trans N.P. Milner (1993). Liverpool: Liverpool University Press.

Zosimus, *New History*, trans. R.T. Ridley (1982). Canberra: Australian Association for Byzantine Studies.

Modern works

Atanasov, G. (2014). 'The portrait of Flavius Aëtius (390–454) from Durostorum (Silistra) inscribed on a consular diptych from Monza', *Studia Academica Šumenensia* 1: 7–21.

Bóna, I. (1991). *Das Hunnenreich*. Stuttgart: Konrad Theiss Verlag.

Bury, J.B. (1889). *A History of the Later Roman Empire*. Two volumes. London & New York, NY: Macmillan & Co.

Creasy, E. (1851). *Fifteen Decisive Battles of the World: from Marathon to Waterloo*. London: Richard Bentley.

Crump, G. (1975). *Ammianus Marcellinus as a Military Historian*. Historia Zeitschrift für alte Geschichte: Einzelschriften, Heft 27. Wiesbaden: Franz Steiner Verlag.

Delbrück, H., trans. W.J. Renfroe, Jr. (1980). *The Barbarian Invasions* (History of the Art of War Vol. II). Lincoln, NE: University of Nebraska Press. Originally published in German in 1921.

Elton, H. (1996). *Warfare in Roman Europe AD 350–425*. Oxford: Oxford University Press.

Gibbon, E. (1776). *The History of the Decline and Fall of the Roman Empire*. Volume 1. London: W. Strahan & T. Cadell.

Gibbon, E. (1781). *The History of the Decline and Fall of the Roman Empire*. Volume 2. London: W. Strahan & T. Cadell.

Glover, F.M. (1973). 'Geiseric and Attila', *Historia* 22: 104–17.

Heather, P. (1991). *Goths and Romans 332–489*. Oxford: Clarendon Press.

Heather, P. (1995). 'The Huns and the End of the Roman Empire in Western Europe', *The English Historical Review* 110: 4–41.

Heather, P. (2007). *The Fall of the Roman Empire. A New History*. London: Pan.

Hodgkin, T. (1892–96). *Italy and Her Invaders*. Two volumes. Second Edition. Oxford: Clarendon Press.

Howarth, P. (1994). *Attila, King of the Huns. The Man and the Myth*. London: Constable.

Hughes, Ian (2012). *Aëtius: Attila's Nemesis*. Barnsley: Pen & Sword.

Hughes, Ian (2019). *Attila the Hun: Arch-Enemy of Rome*. Barnsley: Pen & Sword.

Jones, A.H.M. (1964). *The Later Roman Empire 284–602*. Two volumes. Norman, OK: University of Oklahoma Press.

Jones, A.H.M, Martindale, J.R. & Morris, J. (1980). *The Prosopography of the Later Roman Empire*, Volume 2. Cambridge: Cambridge University Press.

Kim, Hyun Jin (2016). *The Huns* (Peoples of the Ancient World). London: Routledge.

Maas, M., ed. (2015). *The Cambridge Companion to the Age of Attila*. Cambridge: Cambridge University Press.

Maenchen-Helfen, Otto J. (1973). *The World of the Huns: Studies in Their History and Culture*. Berkeley & Los Angeles, CA: University of California Press.

Man, J. (2005). *Attila. The Barbarian King and the Fall of Rome*. London: Bantam.

Matthews, J. (2007). *The Roman Empire of Ammianus*. Revised edition. Ann Arbor, MI: Michigan Classical Press.

Nicholson, O., ed. (2018). *Oxford Dictionary of Late Antiquity*. Two volumes. Oxford: Oxford University Press.

Schultheis, E.M. (2019). *The Battle of the Catalaunian Fields AD 451*. Barnsley: Pen & Sword Military.

Southern, P. & Dixon, K.R. (1996). *The Late Roman Army*. New Haven, CT: Yale University Press.

Syvänne, I. (2020). *Military History of Late Rome 425–457: The Age of Warlords. Aëtius vs. Attila*. Barnsley: Pen & Sword Military.

Thompson, E.A. (1996). *The Huns* (The Peoples of Europe). London: Wiley-Blackwell.

Wallace-Hadrill, J.M. (1962). *The Long-Haired Kings*. London: Methuen.

INDEX